Understanding the Office and Battles of Every Pastor's Wife

Understanding the Office and Battles of Every Pastor's Wife

What She, Her Husband, and Church Members Need to Know

by Ritabella M. Kunobwa

Purpose House Publishing

Copyright © 2024 Ritabella Kunobwa. All rights reserved.

Published by PurposeHouse Publishing, Columbia, Maryland. Cover Design by PurposeHouse Publishing and David Kunobwa.
Printed in the USA.

No part of this publication may be reproduced or distributed in any form or by any means or stored in a database or retrieval system without the prior written permission of the author.

ISBN: 978-1-957190-17-4

Scripture quotations marked (AMP or AMPC) are taken from the Amplified Bible Copyright 2015 by The Lockman Foundation. Used by permission. All rights reserved.

Scripture quotations marked (CEV) are taken from the Contemporary English Version Used by permission. All rights reserved worldwide.

Scripture quotations marked (GW) are taken from GOD'S WORD®. © 1995, 2003, 2013, 2014, 2019, 2020 by God's Word to the Nations Mission Society. Used by permission.

Scripture quotations marked (KJV) are taken from the Holy Bible, King James Version (Public Domain).

Scripture quotations marked (NIV) are from the New International Version, Copyright © 1973, 1978, 1984 by Biblica.

Scripture quotations marked (NKJV) are taken from the New King James Version®, Copyright © 1982 by Thomas Nelson. Used by permission. All rights reserved.

Scripture quotations marked (NLT) are taken from the Holy Bible, New Living Translation, copyright © 1996, 2004, 2015 by Tyndale House Foundation.

Scripture quotations marked (Phillips) are taken from The New Testament in Modern English, copyright 1958, 1959, 1960 J.B. Phillips and 1947, 1952, 1955, 1957 The Macmillian Company, New York. Used by permission. All rights reserved.

Dedication

To all pastors' wives working wholeheartedly in the vineyard despite the venomous attacks. May God use this book as an instrument of strength, wisdom, revival, and encouragement. Remember, "God *is* not unjust to forget your work and labor of love which you have shown toward His name, *in that* you have ministered to the saints, and do minister" (Hebrews 6:10 NKJV).

May you continue to rule in the midst of your enemies. May this book also help you to navigate your way in the office of a pastor's wife.

The good Lord bless you, keep you, and make His face shine upon you as you execute your duties in the pastor's wife's office. Shalom.

Contents

Section One: The Office of A Pastor's Wife _____ 1

    Chapter 1: Misconceptions and Controversies: It's Not What You or the Congregation Think _____ 3

    Chapter 2: Extinguishing Flames of Fame _____ 13

    Chapter 3: No Paper or Plastic: A Stabilizing Force _____ 21

    Chapter 4: Overcoming Inferiority Complex: You're God's Choice _____ 33

Section Two: Responsibilities Of Every Pastor's Wife _____ 49

    Chapter 5: Intercession: It Matters if You Pray _____ 51

    Chapter 6: Nurturing: The Art of Spiritual Motherhood _____ 63

    Chapter 7: Dos and Don'ts for Every Pastor's Wife _____ 75

Section Three: Battles Every Pastor's Wife Fights _____ 93

    Chapter 8: Accusations _____ 95

    Chapter 9: Competition _____ 103

    Chapter 10: Dishonor _____ 117

    Chapter 11: Famine _____ 127

    Chapter 12: Gossip and Hypocrisy _____ 135

    Chapter 13: Jezebels _____ 151

    Chapter 14: Loneliness _____ 167

    Chapter 15: Rebellious Children _____ 183

    Chapter 16: Strife and Divide and Rule Members _____ 193

    Chapter 17: Unforgiveness _____ 199

Conclusion _____ 205

Foreword

With immense joy and honor, I introduce you to Understanding the Office and Battles of Every Pastor's Wife, a timely and insightful work authored by Pastor Ritabella Kunobwa. This book explores the critical role of a pastor's wife by offering much-needed wisdom, clarity, and practical counsel for women called to this noble office. It serves as a guide for pastors' wives and congregations seeking to honor and support their wives in their God-given assignments.

I truly believe this book answers the cry and prayer of many pastors' wives. Pastor Ritabella's insights offer them understanding, validation, and practical tools needed to embrace their divine assignments with confidence and uncommon grace. Her words remind them they are specially equipped for their peculiar role in ministry.

I've had the privilege of knowing Pastor Ritabella and her husband, Apostle David Kunobwa, for over a decade through Women Full of Grace International, a Pastors' Wives Network founded by Pastor Dr. Adesuwa Onaiwu. Over the years, I have witnessed Pastor Ritabella's deep commitment and growth in the office of a pastor's wife. Her heart for ministry and her passion for encouraging women who stand beside their husbands in ministry are commendable.

As you read this book, may you be strengthened, encouraged, and equipped to fulfill your calling with grace and empowerment by the Holy Spirit.

Yours in Kingdom Expansion,

Bishop Dr. Nosa Onaiwu
Arise and Shine International Ministries

Acknowledgements

To my Lord and Savior, Jesus Christ, thank you for choosing me out of billions to nurture, mentor, and guide souls into the kingdom of God. I am forever and ever grateful for the privilege and opportunity you have given me to advance your Kingdom.

I extend my sincere gratitude to my husband, the incomparable Dr. David E. Kunobwa, for your support and encouragement to birth this vision into reality. Your faith in me has taken me to heights and dimensions. I am forever grateful that you chose me, gave me a platform, took me to the runway, and encouraged me to fly and soar in the Spirit. May God remember your great contribution to my destiny.

To my four supportive and loving children, thank you for being inspirational. May God lead each of you to the path of destiny He has set for you.

To my spiritual family at Rivers of Life Assembly International in Woburn, MA, thank you for being this book project's case study and triggers.

To my dearest best friend, the late Pastor Gloria Omosigho, the wisdom you instilled is still functional and applicable to the pastor's wife's office. I miss you greatly. May you continue to rest in peace.

To Women Full of Grace International, the home of pastors' wives' conferences at Arise and Shine International, you have contributed enormously to the substance, wisdom, teaching, and impartation of this project. I am forever grateful.

To the late Dr. Adesuwa Onaiwu, the seeds you planted in a young, scared, and intimidated pastor's wife have grown big enough to now speak to this generation of pastors' wives. Your contribution to this project can never be underestimated or forgotten. From the bottom of my heart, I say thank you for the vision that brought me this far. Keep resting in power, mother in Zion.

To Bishop Nosa Onaiwu of Arise and Shine International Ministries in Dallas, Texas, thank you for manning the fort of the pastor's wives' conferences. Your prayers and impartation have not left me the same. I honor and salute you, Bishop. God richly bless you.

To my mother, Rhona, thank you for your contribution to my Christian path. Mom, I don't miss the courts of law at all. I found the place where God ordained me for ministry. God bless and keep you.

To my late father, Elijah K. Mutyabule, Esquire, thank you for investing greatly in my education and shielding me from persecutions that once attempted to stop me from going to papyrus churches. May you keep resting in peace.

Lastly, to the Purpose House Publishing team, thank you for making my vision a reality. I am eternally grateful. God bless and expand your borders and boundaries.

SECTION ONE: THE OFFICE OF A PASTOR'S WIFE

Sarah was not simply consequential to Abraham; she shared in their assignment as a mother of nations (Genesis 17:16). In the same way, a pastor's wife is a mothering co-heir of grace with her husband. It comes with her office, and she must not draw back from it.

This section further explains the office of a pastor's wife. It dispels common misconceptions that current and potential pastor's wives, pastors, and congregation members have about her role. It offers all parties sound wisdom and dos and don'ts concerning the pastor's wife's office. Congregation members will understand how to relate to their pastor's wife with honor and revelation of God's true concept of her role.

In addition, this section (and book) speaks to current and potential husband-pastors. If they are unmarried and praying for a wife, it will help them choose a wife to co-labor with them in ministry. It will help all husband-pastors better understand their wives' roles, how to support them, and specific husband-pastor pitfalls to avoid.

It also addresses the inferiority complex, which plagues many pastor's wives. By embracing the principles and wisdom in this section, pastors' wives will arm themselves with the insight necessary to walk with godly confidence. It will also help them avoid pitfalls and please God while executing their office.

Chapter 1: Misconceptions and Controversies: It's Not What You or the Congregation Think

When you hear the words pastor's wife, what comes to mind?

There are many ideas and misconceptions concerning the office of a pastor's wife, primarily because so many people have varying perspectives on who she should be. Current and prospective husband-pastors have their own desires; some want a wife who can preach; others just want a beautiful wife. Many current and prospective pastors' wives have had no one to train them for the office. They watched other pastors' wives and only formed their opinions of the office from distant observation. In-laws are another party with a set of expectations that are often not biblical. Moreover, church members contribute heavily to the misconceptions and unrealistic expectations of the office. Indeed, each party has their own opinions and visions of who an ideal pastor's wife would be.

However, each party must understand the true concept of a pastor's wife, which is God's original mind and purpose for pastors' wives. A right understanding will enable current and prospective pastors' wives to fulfill their assignments and current husband-pastors to ensure they relate properly to their wives and understand the role they must play in co-laboring with them.

Prospective pastors need a good understanding to choose a future wife well and avoid detrimental consequences. In-laws need understanding to operate with realistic expectations and provide familial support. And church members need understanding to ensure they properly relate to and respect their pastor's wife.

The reality is that a pastor's wife should be a blessing to and impacts all who represent these varying perspectives, so we must address common misconceptions and bring an understanding of the true concept of a pastor's wife.

Our journey begins with the crucial task of dispelling misconceptions. Whether you're a current or prospective husband-pastor, pastor's wife, or a congregation member, it is imperative to dispel myths and set our minds aright concerning this important office. This task cannot be delayed, as it is essential for the health and unity of pastoral marriages, churches, and Kingdom advancement.

Dispelling Misconceptions

The pastor's wife's office is not a fashionista position or beauty showcase.

Many deem the office of a pastor's wife as a position to orchestrate and showcase beauty and fashion. Though these two elements could have played a significant role in earning someone the position, being a pastor's wife is more than fashion and beauty. Even if beauty and fashion opened the door for someone to become a pastor's wife, those elements alone cannot keep them there.

Esther's beauty and wisdom earned her the Queen's position (Esther 2:7, 17). Yet, with all her beauty, the King had not called on her for months before she stood before him unannounced (Esther 5:1-8). It took the power of God to maintain her queenship. So, allow me to submit to every reader of this book that it takes more than beauty and fashion to be a pastor's wife.

When challenging times came during her queenship, Esther had to fast and pray (Esther 4:16). Spiritual activities are necessary to maintain and release something supernatural upon you and give you staying power to bear the weight of the office.

It's more than sitting in the front row.

Like beauty and fashion, some are thrilled over the outward appearance of sitting in the front row on throne-like chairs next to the senior pastor. Esther wasn't seated next to the King when she appeared unannounced. What she had done outside the sanctuary in fasting and prayer empowered her to win in the inner court.

So, it's not about where you sit physically. One of the strengths of a pastor's wife is her ability to influence things from the background. Specifically, her ability to influence things in the realm of the spirit. It's more important to ensure that as a pastor's wife, you're in the heavenly realms with Christ Jesus—in supernatural positions of authority—than occupying the front seat without any oil of the anointing in your life. You must have spiritual status (a seat of authority) in the realm of the spirit.

It's not easy. It's very demanding, and many women battle to reconcile the demands of the office with the misconceptions surrounding this ministry.

The office of the pastor's wife is very demanding if not one of the most demanding ministries. It comes with many battles and challenges, including its many responsibilities and reconciling it with the misconceptions surrounding it. Some of the challenges include:

- A pastor's wife must be understanding when her spouse is away to seek God instead of spending time with her.
- She must share her husband with God, the children, and the church. She is often alone.
- She constantly serves and prepares things for her husband—in the house and the ministry. For example, she cooks for multiple places. She prepares food spiritually and physically for him and the children and must have a deep well on which they can feed. Jacob dug a very deep well to the extent that it watered people when he was gone. Whether she has a five-fold ministry calling or not, a pastor's wife must have a deep well of prayer from which her family can draw.
- Being a pastor's wife is spiritually demanding because she must steer many things in the ministry. In most cases, the pastor's wife can explain the vision to the congregation in her husband's absence because she is the co-driver of the vision. No elder or deacon can explain it better than her in the pastor's absence.
- She's responsible for organizing many things in the ministry; many pastors are not good at organizing and planning.
- She must engage the man of God on sensitive issues because no one else can stand up or be bold enough to tell him that some choices are bad decisions. However, she can because it's her role to tell him what he cannot see. Many women perceive faster than men. For example, in 2 Kings 4:8-9, a wife says to her husband, "Behold now, I perceive that this is an holy man of God, which passeth by us continually" (KJV). The wife perceived that Elisha was a holy man of God, but if the woman had not perceived it, they would have missed their miracle of childbearing.

Likewise, there are many times I can see things ahead of my husband—sometimes a year ahead. Husbands, please remember that when God tells your wife, He has told you. Many men have egos and battle what their wives are saying. It helps if the pastor also understands his wife's ministry; it allows the work to grow faster and quicker.

The pastor's wife must be respected. It is an error to feel that only the pastor needs to be respected. It will not yield a blessing. She is a co-heir of grace.

At this point, allow me to correct every church member, worker, or leader who undermines and underestimates the position of a pastor's wife on the pretext that you and your teammates will stand with your pastor in intercession and usher him into victory. Please understand that before God pays attention to your prayer, He listens and considers the prayer of the pastor's wife because she is in covenant with the man of God. Their marriage is a covenant—not a partnership like others who may come alongside him in the ministry. God honors covenant, and when you understand that, your journey in their ministry will be much easier.

No one should undermine a pastor's wife's authority. 1 Peter 3:7 says, "Similarly, you husbands should try to understand the wives you live with, honouring them as physically weaker *yet equally heirs* with you of the grace of eternal life. If you don't do this, *you will find it impossible to pray properly*" (PHILLIPS, italics added). Husbands and the congregation should honor their wives as equal heirs (co-heirs and joint heirs) so that God does not hinder the husband's prayers. If pastor's wives are not handled with respect, they create hindrances and barriers in the realm of the spirit for the man of God and sometimes the ministry.

So, church members, workers, and team leaders who respect the man of God but not his wife are out of order and need realignment. Exalting the pastor but not respecting or undermining the wife's position means you are undermining a covenant. It is a mistake to think that will attract blessings. Such attitudes attract curses.

Surprisingly, you find many women disrespecting the pastor's wife. Women often look down on other women, which comes from a place of competition. No congregation member should ever feel she would have been a better choice as the pastor's wife. God chose one Eve for every Adam. There may be more beautiful women in the church, but the pastor (and God) did not choose them.

Here are additional crucial reasons you must not dishonor a pastor's wife:

- Many times, the husband is where they are in life and ministry because of the wife's hard work.
- The pastor's wife may also be a five-fold ministry gift who labors in the Word of God and prayer, making her worthy of double honor in her own right according to the Scriptures (1 Timothy 5:17).
- The pastor and the pastor's wife are one team—they are co-heirs. They are not two teams working against each other.

Over ten years ago, something happened in ministry, and I decided to step aside. When I did, the ministry went down; it took a turn for the worse. My husband had gone to minister, and a woman called him out and told him, "You are married to a dynamic woman of God, but you are not with her. And as long as you are not with her, you don't have a ministry." He took it lightly, but when he came home, he had a dream. In the dream, it was as if he was trying to drive up a hill, stepping hard on the accelerator. The car would move forward a bit but go backward on the hill. The Lord told him, "Unless you agree with her, you won't be able to drive over the hill." In the dream, after my husband and I agreed, he was able to drive over the top of the hill and even buy a big house, symbolizing stability and blessing.

When we became a team and agreed to work together, we saw the miracle of that house manifest. We have it now, not because we earned it, but because it's the grace of God and a result of the commanded blessing on unity (Psalm 133:3). There are some blessings a man will never walk in until he is one with his wife. Agreement is particularly important. Amos 3:3 says, "Can two walk together, except they be agreed?" (KJV).

Agreement is the key to unlocking progress in the realm of the spirit and the ministry. Remember, one can chase 1,000, but two can chase 10,000 (Deuteronomy 32:30). Increase comes by partnership; some breakthroughs, elevations, promotions, etc., will only come by partnership with your God-given spouse. So, choose not to delay yourself. Get into agreement and partnership with whoever God has appointed for you to partner with in ministry.

Furthermore, church members or leaders who work tirelessly to turn their pastor against his wife contribute to his downfall, if not stagnancy in his ministry. Believers need to understand it's a pure misconception, lack of understanding, and lack of ministerial ethics and biblical principles to dishonor a pastor's wife while amplifying the man of God. She is in his life to do the checks and balances that not even the best prayer warrior can because she is in covenant with him.

Let's further explore the true concept of a pastor's wife, and we'll understand even more why her husband and the congregation must respect her.

The True and Biblical Concept of a Pastor's Wife

According to the Bible, God made wives helpers or helpmates of husbands. The pastor's wife's marital assignment is to be the God-given helper to her husband. That means there is help that only she can give her husband-pastor, and no prayer warrior, assistant pastor, or church leader's help can substitute. Her position in her husband's life is similar to the ministry of the Holy Spirit, as He is also described as another helper (John 14:16 NKJV).

Women with no capability or capacity are not fit to provide aid or help. Beauty and makeup don't resolve spiritual problems. But God has endowed true wives with capabilities that aid their husbands. A help meet has to be meet or able to do something and meet also means comparable in capacity to him. God never intended a wife to be a simple ornament. She has a function; He divinely appoints pastors' wives to help their husbands fulfill their calling.

That assignment as a helper also highlights the fact that pastors or husbands are not perfect people. They need a wife to help perfect their walk with the Lord and that which concerns their calling and ministries. A pastor must allow his wife to play her vital role; they must both walk in humility. If not, he may find himself vulnerable with no one to tell him the truth.

Many friends and fellow pastors find correcting the man of God hard. I don't blame them because it's not their place. A pastor's wife is the one who should and is in a better position to help her husband regarding his errors and weaknesses. Here are some reasons why:

1. It's her office and her assignment.
2. It's her mission to help him.
3. She knows him better than everyone and is more

interested in seeing him succeed than fail. She has his best interest at heart.
4. She has the grace to help the pastor in all or most aspects.
5. She has a covenant with the man of God. God gives a person who has a covenant preeminence or an upper hand. Before God listens to an intercessor, prayer warrior, or church team member, He listens to the wife first. In Genesis 21:12-13, God instructs Abraham, a man called of God, anointed, and highly favored of God, to listen to his wife. He was telling him to leave God's permissive will and get into God's perfect and covenanted will. (God still emphasized to Abraham that He would even bless Ishmael because he was the seed of a man who had a covenant with Him.) Throughout Scripture, God listens to those with a covenant. Genesis 22:16-17 further highlights this when Hagar wept and lifted her voice, but God was silent. However, as soon as the lad raised his voice, God heard. He dispatched an angel instantly because God had listened to Ishmael's voice. Why Ishmael and not Hagar? Ishmael had a covenant with God through his dad, Abraham.

God uniquely positioned the pastor's wife to help her husband avoid embarrassment. It's difficult to tell the pastor things about his personal hygiene or judge his sermon, but his wife can discuss such things without any harmful intentions. She's helping him improve by addressing sensitive issues nobody else may be able to—not even his mother. A husband leaves his mother and cleaves to his wife. So, if the mother can't help him, the wife must step up and help him.

The pastor must also be willing to listen. Four women may play a vital role in a man's life: his mother, sister, daughter, and wife. He will have to listen to one of them at some point in life. For example, T.D. Jakes has said that his daughter, Sarah Jakes, has the boldness to speak into his life, and he actually appreciates that. But why not let your wife play her God-given role?

A pastor may listen to intercessors or some church members who seem anointed, but the Bible says his prayers will be hindered if he does not listen to his wife (1 Peter 3:7). Her voice must be respected and honored more than the so-called anointed intercessors in the church. God will listen to those who have a covenant.

Here is another word of caution regarding the office of a pastor's wife. Genesis 2:18 stipulates that pastors' wives are helpers, not competitors or threats to their husbands. Congregation members can sometimes compare the ministries of wives who are anointed ministry gifts to their husbands'. Sometimes, a wife is more anointed or has a stronger grace than her husband. Or the husband may be lazy in prayer. In that case, the anointing may land on the more prayerful woman, and people begin to request the wife's ministry more than the husband. Without care, the ministry can stir up strife. The husband, wife, and congregation need to know the two of them are not competing. They are co-heirs; they are one team. There should be no competition, whether initiated by immature congregation members or in the hearts of the husband or wife.

In the next chapter, we address the pastor's wife's battle with the "flames of fame," and learn what every pastor's wife's focus in ministry should be.

Chapter 2: Extinguishing Flames of Fame

"Seekest thou great things for thyself? seek them not . . ." – God speaking to Baruch in Jeremiah 45:5a KJV

Many parents have warned young children not to touch fire, whether on a stove or from matches. Still, a child's foolish curiosity provokes them to touch the fire, and they cry painfully from the burn. So it is with the "flames of fame." Many people desire notoriety; they want the spotlight until they enter the stage under the bright lights and realize they burn.

Some pastor's wives have burned to ashes under the spotlight because they were ill-warned and ill-prepared. Many had little or limited exposure to the public before they married a pastor. No one warned them that becoming a pastor's wife moves your life from the shadows to the spotlight—at least in the church community. Few are comfortable or even prepared to live a public life.

Mistakes are common when a pastor's wife is less prepared or does not know how to handle public attention, and the size of the church does not matter. Many need help dealing with or handling fame on both a small and large scale. A pastor's wife will always be a pastor's wife, whether the church is big or small.

Fame is not easy. It comes with jealousy, envy, and attempts of sabotage. While glamorous from the outside, it is often lonely on the inside. And if a pastor's wife suffered rejection before assuming her office, that rejection only magnifies and can do lots of damage, affecting how she handles the office and adding to her peril in the flames of fame.

To better prepare pastor's wives, bring awareness, and inform their husbands and congregations, I discuss some perils of the "flames of fame."

Your private life can burn to ashes in the flames of fame.

The congregation focuses on the lives of the pastor and his wife. They place high expectations on their marriage and even criticize them for the same ills they experience in their own marriages. They inspect them and their children's appearance with a microscope; they put them under the spotlight.

Even worse, they expect access to their pastor and, sometimes, to his home all day and night. There may be times when a pastor's wife comes home to find a team leader in her house, goes to church to meet church members for Bible study, waits long periods after church to talk to members on Sundays, receives phone calls late in the night, fields questions from her children about where daddy is and when he's coming home, and has to run her own aspects of the ministry. This can be overwhelming for a quiet, private person who did not grow up with lots of people in the house. So, many pastors' wives are shocked when they are suddenly in the limelight, and their former private, quiet manner of living is destroyed.

They may feel they have no room to breathe and isolate themselves to protect their private lives. Members may begin to say she is aloof and unfriendly when she is only trying to keep her privacy and sanity. Everyone should take care to balance the congregation's access to the pastor and his home, and the husband-pastor must prioritize and plan time with his family.

Your modesty and purity can burn to ashes in the flames of fame.

The pastor's wife's dress code is always a center of attention for church members and is a make-or-break issue. A pastor's wife who does not have proper training or exposure on how to handle the flames of fame can be tempted to turn her office into a platform for her personal fashion show. She diminishes her vital role to mere "show business" instead of becoming a role model of decency and appropriate Christian attire. The women in the house—old and young—will look to the pastor's wife's manner of dressing as a model. Thus, as the mother of a congregation, a pastor's wife cannot be careless about her dress code. It is a huge mistake for a pastor's wife to use her platform to parade her personal fashion. Instead, she should use her dress code to mold (shape) and lead a generation.

She should not dress like a teenager or in any other inappropriate manner, especially on the pulpit. I always tell my church daughters I have all the so-called fashionista attire to wear, but the problem is wearing them to church in the pulpit—that is the wrong place. For example, someone should not wear beach attire in the pulpit. That is not the right attire for church, as much as it may look very pretty. Obviously, someone should not wear summer clothes in the deep winter even if they look good. It is the same principle. Some pastors' wives need to recover from the flames of fame and remember they are in their position to imitate Christ. Pastor's wife, as you choose your clothes for church, always remember the next generation is looking up to you.

A daughter will not be comfortable doing things in her home that she never saw her mother do in her home. Likewise, a pastor's wife will always be the role model other women and future pastors' wives in the congregation look to (especially new pastors' wives). If the pastor's wife is not decent, the children and spiritual children will not be decent; they will spread the virus of indecency wherever they go.

For example, a few years ago, someone joined our church after leaving a big church. We initially gave her opportunities to minister, but her dress code was always an abomination. She said her former pastor's wife dressed that way. This exemplifies why a pastor's wife's dress code is a make-or-break issue. She will reproduce after her own kind.

That sister who we gave chances to minister refused correction and eventually left the church. She has not achieved much or been able to go far because her style is about showing off her body and not Christ in her, who is the hope of glory (Colossians 1:27).

The generational standards may have changed, but godly standards will never change. "Sexy" has never been fashion for the pulpit; it's for married people in the bedroom. In ancient days, women did not show cleavage, shoulders, and thighs. Now, they do, and the dresses are so tight. Nonetheless, according to the standards of God's Word, it is not okay. In 1 Timothy 2:9, Paul says, "I also want the women to dress modestly, with decency and propriety, adorning themselves, not with elaborate hairstyles or gold or pearls or expensive clothes" (NIV). Beloved, it is not okay for a pastor's wife to dress like she's going to a nightclub or the beach and step into the pulpit.

Jesus identified someone with the wrong dress code, and they cast him away. "He asked, 'How did you get in here without wedding clothes, friend?' The man was speechless. Then the King told the attendants, 'Tie him hand and foot, and throw him outside, into the darkness, where there will be weeping and gnashing of teeth'" (Matthew 22:12-13 NIV). The attendants cast him away because of his garments, which are important. An ungodly dress code can earn you a ticket to hell; it's okay to come as you are, but you cannot stay as you are.

So, why would any pastor's wife want to mount the pulpit without the right attire? What you wear and how you present yourself as a preacher or pastor's wife is important. People from all walks of life are looking at you. You either point them in the right or wrong direction.

Accept it or not, you either manifest the devil or Jesus Christ in your dress code—not both. If you dress to show your body, remember you're attracting people to you and not Christ—you're driving them to the gates of hell. For example, if you are married and you still dress to attract men, you will lead people to lust after you. In so doing, they will not fall in love with Jesus. Instead, you will become a hindrance to them seeing Christ's light. I recall a vivid example of this truth.

Once, at a singles ministry dinner, my husband and I sat at a table with other church members, and a sister showed up with her breasts falling out of her dress. One brother could not eat because of her attire. I could tell this brother was having a tough time because he kept going to the bathroom. We suspect he might have masturbated because of that sister's dress code. Her dress code became a stumbling block for the brother. Just a few weeks later, that brother fell into sexual sin and did not return to church. No believer, pastor's wife or not, should ever want to cause anybody to fall.

So the question is, was there no spiritual mother to help this woman? If a young pastor's wife doesn't get their dress code right, it's often because their spiritual mother is not helping them.

God will hold pastors' wives accountable for misleading the next generation in this area. We don't dress to seduce but to lead people to Christ. You never lead any man to Christ if you're a woman preaching with your breasts showing or exposed. You will be inviting them to yourself—not to Christ. You will be leading them to the gates of hell—not the gates of heaven.

Pastor's wives must do a "Holy Ghost check" in the mirror before heading to church. When I say a "Holy Ghost check," I mean, asking the Holy Ghost to confirm whether you attire passes the scans and standards of the Kingdom of God?

This reminds me of a guest I once hosted. She was expecting me to dress indecently because, according to her, everyone in the US does. I didn't know she had been observing my dress code. She said, "Oh, for a while, I have noticed you dress decently. Why, when you live in the US?" I told her, "I am in the world but not of this world. I don't want to be accountable for anyone's downfall." This should be every believer's desire and much more a pastor's wife. Note what Jesus said in the following passage.

> If anyone causes one of these little ones—those who believe in me—to stumble, it would be better for them to have a large millstone hung around their neck and to be drowned in the depths of the sea. (Mathew 18:6 NIV)

Your focus on your heavenly calling can burn to ashes in the flames of fame.

Every pastor's wife must avoid the peril of having a wrong focus. Instead, she must focus on her true assignment, or fame will easily carry her away. She will wrongly focus on the benefits of her office rather than the assignment.

Pastor's wife, proceed with caution. Be careful not to let people carrying your bag or Bible puff you up because God will hold you accountable. Man looks at the outward appearance, but God looks at the heart. He requires fruit from your office.

You and I will have to give an account to Jesus. When He shows up, it will not be about social media likes but who you have nurtured, matured, and discipled—whose life you have built and are developing. This is the right focus for the pastor's wife. She must ask herself if she's building people's prayer lives, faith, and spiritual development or just destroying things in the ministry and at home. She must ask herself if she's uplifting and nurturing the children God has invested in her hands. Those are the key takeaways from your office and assignment. It is the fruit God desires. Without a proper focus, this fruit will perish in the flames of fame.

The next chapter discusses the character and maturity necessary to produce this fruit and become a stabilizing force as a pastor's wife.

Chapter 3: No Paper or Plastic: A Stabilizing Force

"Therefore whoever hears these sayings of Mine, and does them, I will liken him to a wise man who built his house on the rock." – Jesus in Matthew 7:24 NKJV

If God entrusts you with the pastor's wife's office, you must be a rock. You cannot be a paper or plastic woman easily destroyed by the fire every ministry on Earth must endure. Most, if not all, pastors' wives go through the fire—times of great challenges and tests. Therefore, you must be able to withstand the battles that come with the office. You are the raw material God wants to use to build His Kingdom, and He wants to build on rocks, not sand.

Rocks can survive winds, floods, and fire, but plastic and paper cannot—not even for as little as two minutes. Matthew 7:24-25 says, ". . . which built his house upon a rock: And the rain descended, and the floods came, and the winds blew, and beat upon that house; and it fell not: for it was founded upon a rock" (KJV). So, to be a pastor's wife and withstand the floods and waves of ministry, you must be a rock that God can use to build a solid foundation and support for the ministry.

You must be a fire-resistant Christian. That means a pastor's wife must have a gossip-proof character. She must have a character made of trouble-resistant material, so she continues to stand no matter what comes her way.

A pastor's wife may feel inadequate, but when God chooses her, He doesn't look at the outside; He's more focused on what she's carrying on the inside. Some women are so interested in being or becoming a pastor's wife, but they are plastic. They are not rocks in their character. God cannot and will not build using that material. Other women may have been competitors, but He cannot trust a woman with plastic or paper character with the pastor's wife's office because they are bound to do more harm than good.

God can trust a rock, not a paper woman, because a rock doesn't change with the weather. Paper and plastic change; they can lose their shape or form easily. When the weather changes in ministry, you must still be strong enough to move forward with your vision and calling, refusing to let God down because He trusted you with the office.

Who has ever seen a foundation built using plastic material? It's a misconception when plastic women want rock positions. A builder can only build a foundation well using rocks or stones. If anyone makes the mistake of building a foundation with plastic materials, they can rest assured that what they build will not last. However, if you want to build something that will last for many generations, use the right people in your foundation.

Peter, Our Example

Peter helps us understand the kind of rocks pastors' wives need to be. After Peter declared that Jesus was the Christ, the Son of the living God, Jesus told him, "Flesh and blood hath not revealed it unto thee, but my Father which is in heaven . . . and upon this rock I will build my church; and the gates of hell shall not prevail against it" (Matthew 16:17-18 KJV). Your strength as a rock is in your focus on Jesus, the rock of our salvation.

God could not use other women because they are not rocks—their focus is on being fashionistas and acquiring fame. He found that you are a rock strong enough to withstand the battles that come with this office. That's why you are the Peter upon which God will build the church, and the gates of hell will not prevail.

> And Jesus answered and said unto him, Blessed art thou, Simon Barjona: for flesh and blood hath not revealed it unto thee, but my Father which is in heaven. And I say also unto thee, That thou art Peter, and upon this rock I will build my church; and the gates of hell shall not prevail against it. (Matthew 16:17-18 KJV)

Why wouldn't Christ build on the other apostles? Maybe they were not rocks. Peter was a rock. That's why, throughout the book of Acts, we see that he went through prison but still stood. He was a rock; thus, he did not break under pressure. Circumstances did not easily discourage him, regardless of what he went through in the ministry. Jesus did not establish the church on a breakable foundation but on sure revelation and determination. He established it on a rock.

A rock is trustable, reliable, and dependable; in other words, just like Peter, whose name means "petra" or rock. God has found you dependable and a good foundation upon which He could lay the ministry. God did not build you to break but to withstand any challenge in ministry. You are immovable. Even if you don't feel like it, God has trusted you anyway.

Like Gideon, you may have some challenges from your background, someone who spoke negatively over your life, or some physical disability like Moses, who stuttered. It doesn't matter; the fact that God chose you means His power can transform you. He can use you for His glory.

Rocks do not break easily; they can withstand any climatical condition. They don't change merely because the weather changes. If you are a Christian who changes your stand with God and the gospel every now and then, you must know God wants you to be a rock not sand.

Pressure moves sand easily, but rocks are immovable. If you're moveable and have no clear stand with the Lord, you're not yet a rock. So, God cannot yet depend on you to build the church. However, just as the Holy Spirit transformed Peter from someone who denied the Lord three times, His power can also transform you into a rock.

In Acts 5:12, Roman guards throw Peter in prison, but he is unkillable and unstoppable. The situation cannot crush him because rocks are not affected by climatic conditions. When it's summer, the heat does not affect the rock. It doesn't melt. When it's winter, you can't freeze it either.

Being a rock does not exempt you from challenges. As much as Peter was a rock, he faced the challenge of being in prison. Through intercession, he broke out of prison and continued with God's mandate for his life. Prayer is vital to the pastor's wife's life and ministry. Even rocks go through challenges, but with much prayer and intercession, the rock will always prevail and remain a rock.

The enemy persecuted and imprisoned Peter. However, because he was solid, that did not affect his stand in the Lord. He continued in God's work. The devil was after him because he was a foundational apostle and powerful. Ask yourself why the other apostles didn't go through what he went through. It's because they didn't have what Peter had in the spirit.

Peter is not here today, but he transferred his mantle to other saints. He imparted that rock-like spirit, and that is why we have people today who are resilient and determined to continue no matter what comes their way. They are still zealous for the Lord through persecution and imprisonment. I received the impartation to be a foundation so that God can build His church upon me, and the gates of hell will not conquer me, in Jesus' name. As you are reading, receive an impartation to be a rock—not plastic material that easily melts when the heat goes up in ministry. You will not faint at the appearance of a trial, test, or challenge. You will stand strong.

That means pastors should choose their wives very wisely. Should any pastor take a wife with a plastic character, his ministry might not last or go far.

Caution to Pastors: The Dangers of Not Choosing a Rock

When you have a ministry calling or are destined to serve God, one way the devil can sabotage you is getting you to marry the wrong person. When a pastor marries wrongly, the foundation of their ministry is faulty because a pastor's wife is one of God's raw materials to build upon. So, if she is not the right one, it affects the foundation. The person who should be able to help build a life and ministry will not withstand the weight that a foundation should.

My kind advice to all pastors is to choose their spouses wisely. Don't only look at her body and outward appearance. I know bodies are attractive and enticing, but bodies are only good for the night—the ministry lasts from generation to generation.

So, before you say I do, scan your bride spiritually. Make sure you ask the Holy Spirit to x-ray them for you. Otherwise, I've seen many men of God limited, broken, blocked, hindered, sabotaged, and adversely affected by the wrong choice they made when choosing a spouse.

Above all, I want to remind you that marriage is a spiritual process, and God should be very involved. Many people take God out of the process when making marital choices. They say, "It's my choice; it's about what I want." However, make sure your choice is God's choice. Otherwise, you'll suffer repercussions.

God's purpose for marriage was spiritual from the beginning, but many pastors are led by the flesh instead of the Holy Spirit when it comes to marriage. As we know, the fruits produced by the flesh are not good. God's process of putting Adam in a deep sleep and extracting Eve from his rib is a sign that only God can give you the right wife, and it will take God to help you make the right choice. So, when you take God out of the equation, you've given Satan an open door to steal, kill, and destroy your ministry.

For example, I know a very anointed man who not only waited a long time to get married but also kept himself pure. One day, a lady walked into his office for counseling. She was exceptionally beautiful to behold, with a perfect complexion, body size, and beautiful hair. She was the kind that would stop traffic without lifting a finger. In an instant, her appearance left the man of God slain and in lust, and he started an affair with her.

He took God out of the equation; he was driven by his desires to get engaged to her after only a few weeks. I'm sure he did not ask God or pray enough about it. He forgot about all the years he had been waiting on God and how big a ministry he had built. Within two months, they were married. I'm sure it was not because God said so but because his emotions compelled him. He was strongly attracted to her sexually, which created a soul tie.

Remember, when you're in ministry, spiritual attraction, not sexual attraction, must be present because sexual attraction in marriage will go away, especially after some time. But spiritual attraction will help you continue the vision you started. So, it is key when venturing into marriage.

This man of God fell from grace to grass because this lady was not about ministry—at all. She was worldly; she was the kind that could not keep only one sex partner. He did not marry his kind in the realm of the spirit, and it affected and sabotaged his ministry.

She continued seeing her ex-boyfriend after marrying the man of God. She also continued her old habits of drinking, clubbing, and dating other married men. She was beautiful, but she did not have the character or capacity it takes to be a pastor's wife. This man of God focused on beauty, but what else did he gain except mental and emotional problems?

The marriage caused him a lot of traumas. He could no longer focus on the ministry; he had no peace. His prayer life diminished, and he was weighed down.

Unfortunately, he has not recovered to being the great man of God I once knew. You can tell the glory departed, and the enemy used one door—the wrong wife. The man of God lost his mantle, influence, and good reputation. Ministerial doors closed for this man because everyone knew the troubles in his home. He fell from being an extraordinary man of God to an ordinary fellow in ministry.

His realm shifted from glory to shame, from supernatural to very natural. He lost many members, and the church God gave him is dormant and almost dead. So, the saying is true: You may marry who you want, but the repercussions are yours to bear if you don't choose wisely with God's guidance.

I beseech every pastor, by God's mercies, to scan the woman you're about to marry spiritually more than physically. Check them out spiritually; investigate their spiritual DNA and background. Believe God to show you the future before you say I do. Otherwise, poor decisions and judgment will destroy your ministry.

Remember, a Delilah, Jezebel, or Hagar can never be a rock. They may look like one, but they are not, and after a careful spiritual scan, you'll tell the difference between a Jezebel and a Deborah. In the same way Satan can masquerade as an angel of light, his agents do as well. Delilahs can appear to be Deborahs because they know how to pretend. They can kneel, salute, and even become your personal assistants or choir leaders but with a demonic agenda. Man of God, be very alert spiritually and keep your spiritual antennas above your physical desires.

I have heard uncountable stories of pastors' ministries destroyed or pulled down because of the way their wives handled things during troublesome times in their ministries. Once, a pastor's wife who suspected that her husband was seeing a young, beautiful lady in the church did much damage. After she got some proof that her husband's infidelity might be true, she picked up the microphone at the end of a Sunday service while everyone watched and warned the young lady to leave her husband alone or she would be dealt with accordingly. After the church witnessed such an obnoxious confrontation, everyone left the ministry. The wife had exposed their pastor's weakness from the pulpit.

This clearly portrays that this pastor's wife was not a rock but a plastic material. She was misplaced by being put into a position of responsibility that only rocks can sustain or manage. I understand it's very annoying for a pastor to engage in such adulterous activities and continue with the ministry's work. However, the fact that she could not go through the fire without involving the entire church was very immature and unethical.

Things would have been better handled if only the wife had been a rock. The congregants should not, at any point, turn into their pastor's marriage counselors. It makes matters complicated. They should not be involved in such matters.

When a pastor's wife is a rock, she goes through these kinds of fires and emerges as a conqueror. She can withstand the fire without involving the congregation. But those who are plastic in nature melt quickly and let their private marital matters find their way into the congregation. As a result, they cause ministry crises or irreparable damages.

For these reasons and more, every pastor needs a spouse with the stabilizing characteristics of a rock, not plastic or paper. Moreover, it is essential to identify the differences and for current and prospective pastors' wives to examine themselves.

Self-Evaluation: Paper, Plastic, or Rock?

Ponder the following table.

Are you or your prospective wife a paper, plastic, or rock kind of woman? Please take a minute to examine yourself.

Character of a Paper or Plastic	Character of Rock
Gossips about issues	Takes issues into intercession
Cannot withstand and falls into the temptation to quit	Withstands and overcomes the temptation to quit

Character of a Paper or Plastic	Character of Rock
Retaliates against competitive women	Remains focused on the vision and mission; she's not built for competition
Doesn't last; melts when the spiritual temperature increases in the ministry	Durable; endures under fire, leaves a legacy, and passes on the baton
Puts up appearances; they appear better than a rock because they look smooth and beautiful, but they are not strong enough to have the capacity to build	May not look that attractive, but they have the spiritual capability and capacity to build, sustain, and support the ministry through it all
Self-centered, self-seeking	Self-sacrificing, seeks others' best interests
Not Kingdom focused; no long-term vision	Kingdom focused; ability to see the greater vision; they are not just short-term but long-term thinkers and have a vision for the future
Kingdom destroyer; a liability in the ministry; allows her reactions to her husband's flaws to destroy the ministry	Kingdom builder; an asset in the ministry even in the face of personal challenges or adversities; does not seek to destroy the ministry because of her husband's flaws
No spiritual substance; they focus on perfumes, colognes, and other material things	Has spiritual substance; they fast, pray, and seek God; they are hungry for God
Not trustworthy; not strong enough to support what the man of God is carrying	Trustworthy because they are strong enough to carry the vision (Proverbs 31:11 KJV)
Beautiful but lacks wisdom	They may not have the most beautiful body, but they have the wisdom to execute kingdom agendas and mandates
Pray and praise only when things are moving well, when the weather is good in the ministry	Pray and praise throughout all weather in the ministry, whether it's hot or cold they don't change

Using the table, you can identify where you or someone else stand as a pastor's wife. Remember, it is only a dead person who cannot adjust. If you have the breath of life, you can change and become a rock that God can use to build and establish the Kingdom.

Do not negate the work of God in your hands.

I have been through so much as a pastor's wife, but I will never forget the very last words of my late spiritual mother, Dr. Adesuwa Onaiwu, of Arise and Shine International Ministries (ASIM) of Bedford, Texas. She said, "No matter the circumstances, do not negate the work of God in your hands."[1] She charged me not to do anything that would destroy the work of God that He entrusted in my hands through my husband. She also said, "You are dealing with souls here, and should you mess up, some people will stumble forever out of the church and out of salvation. God will hold you accountable because He called you to build the Kingdom, not destroy it. Remember, ". . . thou art Peter, and upon this rock I will build my church; and the gates of hell shall not prevail against it" (Matthew 16:18 KJV).

I say to my fellow pastor's wives that I know many times it's difficult in ministry, in the home, and in the family, but purpose to be a Kingdom builder, not a destroyer. It was God who trusted you with that man, so even when you're upset, make decisions that will not cause God to regret giving you that man or trusting you more than other women. Trust God for the grace not to disappoint Him or make Him regret you being a pastor's wife like He regretted having made Saul king (1 Samuel 15:11). Instead,

---

[1] Dr. Adesuwa Onaiwu, Arise and Shine International Ministries (ASIM), Bedford, Texas, https://www.asimglobal.org/pastor-adesuwa-onaiwu.html.

arise and make God proud that He chose you for that work like He was proud of Job (Job 1:8).

I pray that God will not regret making or choosing you and I as pastors' wives. May the almighty God brag about you, in Jesus' name.

The next chapter focuses on overcoming the inferiority complex. In addition to misconceptions and flames of fame, the inferiority complex is a battle that every pastor's wife must overcome to effectively take her position in the pastor's wife's office.

Chapter 4: Overcoming Inferiority Complex: You're God's Choice

"Do not say, 'I am a youth,' For you shall go to all to whom I send you, And whatever I command you, you shall speak." – God to Jeremiah in Jeremiah 1:7 NKJV

An inferiority complex involves a persistent feeling of unworthiness, making someone feel they don't measure up or are not good enough for a person, position, or an assignment. These are feelings of worthlessness—feeling low, undeserving, and having low or no self-esteem. The inferiority complex has stopped many people from going far in the dimensions of God.

Through study and much observation, I have realized that most, if not all, pastors' wives battle low self-esteem at some point in their journey. This gives the devil the advantage to cripple their golden destinies. They cannot dream new dreams or focus on ministry. They cannot function in the fullness of their potential because they don't believe in themselves. They don't feel they are good enough but that others are more suitable candidates for the position.

Inferiority complex causes destiny assassination and must be overcome. So, let's identify and understand some causes of the inferiority complex.

Causes of the Inferiority Complex

For some, childhood experiences damaged their self-esteem. For example, they could have been looked down upon when growing up because they were born last. Family members may have never considered their suggestions and opinions. More specifically, childhood trauma could be the root cause. For example, overly strict or religious parents, peer pressure, teasing, sibling rivalry, or abuse. Specifically, they could've been abused as children because they were stepchildren.

Yet, for others, the cause may be social disadvantages like gender or low socioeconomic status. This includes growing up in a poor home or community. Another example is not being educated or having a degree. Or society may have never respected them because they were women.

For others, the cause may be physical challenges, including weight, height, vision, speech, facial or body features, or a lack of strength. No matter the cause, the inferiority complex always seems to follow us into adulthood, and for many, it follows them until they breathe their last breath.

God gives us life challenges that require us to get out of our comfort zones. If we take these challenges on, we can break free of this terrible bondage. Pastors' wives must be brave enough to take up these challenges.

Unlike pastors, who, most of the time, are aware of what they are getting themselves into with ministry, pastors' wives are either blissfully ignorant or take the matter at hand lightly. They get into marriage with a minister, assuming that they will either only take a backseat, lurk in the shadows, or present themselves only when necessary.

When they finally settle into the marriage, realize that they bit off more than they can chew, and can no longer go back, they clutch all the straws in sight for survival as all their insecurities come to light. They think thoughts like, "But I'm only thirty years old, and the average age of the congregation is forty." Or "I'm neither educated nor eloquent." Or "How can I even match up to the pastor? I can't even come close to being just as good at this as he is."

Why? In addition to a pastor's wife's own insecurities, the inferiority complex is worsened by church members who feel they are better (choristers, ushers, and greeters alike). They feel they could do a better job if they were married to the pastor.

It is also worsened by unsupportive husbands, some who are even abusive behind closed doors. If not physically abused, some pastor's wives are battered by their husband's egos. Such husbands make everything in the ministry about "them," not about "us." They even tell their wives things like, "You know your weaknesses. You know what people are saying about you; you're not good enough. Leave it to someone else, or don't even show up." Such abuse has many pastors' wives' lives constantly affected by the inferiority syndrome. They are battered, bruised, and left without an ounce of confidence to perform their duties as pastors' wives.

Another thing that perpetuates the syndrome is church gossip. Some pastor's wives are not strong enough to withstand church members' gossip or take criticism. Their confidence is already battered, so they get crippled by gossip and tend to stay away from things in the ministry, their duties, and their office. Some run away and leave their assistants to run the ministry or delegate the work to other church members.

Then there are those who directly compete with the pastor's wife. These ladies observe every dress the pastor's wife has, the website she got it from, and go buy the same things. This is direct competition—a competitive spirit in operation. They want to show they can dress better and look better than the pastor's wife.

That can become a big distraction to the pastor's wife who is not prepared for this battle; she must remain focused. Otherwise, she will end up shopping more to compete and try and look just as good. If she has not defined her identity in Christ Jesus, she will be stuck and hindered by the inferiority complex because they're always women whose target is to outdo the pastor's wife. They carry the yoke of, "I know more. I know better." That puts the pastor's wife in a position of being subdued to this syndrome. Further, some members in the ministry are good at showing you or rubbing it in that you're not good enough for their pastor, or they can be better pastor's wives. That leaves many pastors' wives doubtful and unsure about who put them in their position.

My message to a pastor's wife battling with such women who are competitive devils in human form is God saw those so-called "I can be a better pastor's wife" individuals who downplay your role and ability, but He still chose you. Just like God still chose Moses even though Moses himself looked at Aaron as a better choice for the job or assignment. He was eloquent, and Moses was the opposite. Understand that some people may be better than you outwardly, but they are not God's choice for the assignment. They are better in the sense that they assist you where you are weak. Aaron's strength was for Moses' benefit.

My message to other women in the congregation is being better than your pastor's wife does not mean that God called you to be above her. Use your gifts in service to God and your pastor's wife.

Dearest pastor's wife, please don't bow your head to submit to those gifted for your sake (to assist you). For the sake of Moses' ministry, Aaron was eloquent. For the sake of Moses's assignment, he was a mouthpiece. But with all his gifts, he was the assistant, not the leader (Exodus 4:10-15). Congregation member, you can be gifted and still serve under the pastor's wife, not over her.

Inferiority Complex in the Bible

Pastor's wife, rest assured that you are not the first to deal with the inferiority complex. Let's look at some biblical examples of the inferiority complex and the lessons we can learn from them.

Jeremiah

> The word of the LORD came to me, saying, [5] "Before I formed you in the womb I knew you, before you were born I set you apart; I appointed you as a prophet to the nations." [6] "Alas, Sovereign LORD," I said, "I do not know how to speak; I am too young." [7] But the LORD said to me, "Do not say, 'I am too young.' You must go to everyone I send you to and say whatever I command you. [8] Do not be afraid of them, for I am with you and will rescue you," declares the LORD. (Jeremiah 1:4-8 NIV)

In verses four and five, God tells Jeremiah he's appointed as a prophet to the nations. In verse six, Jeremiah responds, "Alas, Sovereign Lord," he says, "I do not know how to speak; I am too young." Jeremiah's inferiority complex was caused by physical challenges. He felt too young to advise others and not eloquent enough to speak. You may also feel too young, or that you've not mastered the art of public speaking, or are not eloquent enough to be a pastor's wife. But remember, it's not about eloquence of speech but the demonstration of power. In 1 Cor. 2:**1**-4, Paul says,

"And my speech and my preaching *were* not with persuasive words of human wisdom, but in demonstration of the Spirit and of power" (NKJV). It's the power of God that makes a difference in people's lives. God used Jeremiah despite his impediment, and He can do the same with you.

In verse five, God says, "Before I formed you in the womb I knew you, before you were born, I set you apart" (Jeremiah 1:5 NIV). God knows our journey before it begins. Therefore, as He says in verse eight, we should not be afraid for He is with us, and He will rescue us. God cannot give you more than you can bear or what you cannot bear on your own. He is always there to make up the difference. Verses nine and ten say, "The Lord reached out His hand and touched my mouth and said to me, "I have put my words in your mouth. See, today I appoint you over nations and kingdoms to uproot and tear down, to destroy and overthrow, to build and to plant." God knows our weaknesses before we are even aware of them, and He has made a provision to turn those weaknesses into strengths.

Gideon

> "Pardon me, my lord," Gideon replied, "but if the LORD is with us, why has all this happened to us? Where are all his wonders that our ancestors told us about when they said, 'Did not the LORD bring us up out of Egypt?' But now the LORD has abandoned us and given us into the hand of Midian." [14] The LORD turned to him and said, "Go in the strength you have and save Israel out of Midian's hand. Am I not sending you?" [15] "Pardon me, my lord," Gideon replied, "but how can I save Israel? My clan is the weakest in Manasseh, and I am the least in my family."
> [16] The LORD answered, "I will be with you, and you will

strike down all the Midianites, leaving none alive."
¹⁷ Gideon replied, "If now I have found favor in your eyes, give me a sign that it is really you talking to me. (Judges 6:13-17 NIV)

During Gideon's day, the Israelites did evil in the eyes of the Lord, and for seven years, He gave them into the hands of the Midianites. In verse fourteen, the angel of the Lord tells Gideon, "Go in the strength you have and save Israel out of Midian's hand. Am I not sending you?" Gideon responds, "Pardon me, my lord, but how can I save Israel? My clan is the weakest in Manasseh, and I am the least in my family."

Gideon's inferiority complex was caused by socioeconomic status and family background. He described his tribe as the weakest and himself as the least of the weakest. You may also see yourself as weak, but God appointed and anointed you. It's not about you or your background but what God can do through you.

Gideon said his father's house was the poorest. Some people had a very poor upbringing and a bad foundation when they were growing up, which affects their self-esteem. As much as God is telling them He will open doors and use them, when they remember where they are coming from, it affects their self-esteem. In Judges 6:16, The Lord answered, "I will be with you, and you will strike down all the Midianites, leaving none alive."

God doesn't even acknowledge what Gideon said. He didn't start up a conversation about his clan or his family because it wasn't important. It was neither a qualifier nor a disqualifier. Sometimes, we give our backgrounds and circumstances more attention than they are worth, and we completely take our focus off the mission at hand. Let's not focus on all those insecurities and pay attention to the fact that God is with us when we pursue the great call that

He has on our lives, and we shall not only be victorious, but we shall do exploits.

In verse seventeen, there is another lesson to learn. Gideon says, "If now I have found favour in your eyes, give me a sign that it is really you talking to me." Gideon was bold enough to ask God for a sign, and God gave him the sign that he needed. It is okay to ask God for a sign, and it is also okay to expect God to give you a sign. After all, isn't He the God of miracles, signs, and wonders? Have bold conversations with God, and you will be surprised how much doing so will build your confidence.

Moses

> Moses said to the LORD, "Pardon your servant, Lord. I have never been eloquent, neither in the past nor since you have spoken to your servant. I am slow of speech and tongue." [11] The LORD said to him, "Who gave human beings their mouths? Who makes them deaf or mute? Who gives them sight or makes them blind? Is it not I, the LORD? [12] Now go; I will help you speak and will teach you what to say." [13] But Moses said, "Pardon your servant, Lord. Please send someone else." [14] Then the LORD's anger burned against Moses and he said, "What about your brother, Aaron the Levite? I know he can speak well. He is already on his way to meet you, and he will be glad to see you. [15] You shall speak to him and put words in his mouth; I will help both of you speak and will teach you what to do. [16] He will speak to the people for you, and it will be as if he were your mouth and as if you were God to him. (Exodus 4:10-16 NIV)

When God appeared to Moses at the burning bush and appointed him to save the Israelites from captivity in Egypt, Moses' inferiority complex came to light and shone more than the bush itself. Even with the full knowledge that God would not only be with him but would help him and teach him what to say, Moses still insisted that God send someone else. This infuriated God. But the Lord knew that the only persuasion left was to give Moses a more qualified partner, Aaron.

There is no shame in needing an Aaron—someone who can help boost your morale or help you deal with things that you are not physically or academically qualified to deal with. Sometimes, that is the strength you need to go forth and answer the Lord's call. This Aaron may be your spouse, worship team, interpreter, intercessors, or ushers, to mention a few. I personally believe that every member of the church is called to help advance the ministry of God. Every member of the church should, in some part, be an Aaron.

God sends Moses help, overlooks his speech impediment, and affirms him as the right person for the office of deliverer and prophet. So, I want to assure every pastor's wife that when God called you, He saw your weaknesses and inabilities. He knew what you could and could not do, but He chose you anyway. Don't let your impediment make you turn your back on the call of God upon your life. You are still God's choice no matter what and the right candidate to execute the pastor's wife's office.

Don't let the devil use this syndrome against you and cause you to drop the ball by saying you're not good enough. God finds you able and fully charged to execute the office. So, take it on, and man it in Jesus' name.

You are God's best! Usually, when you're God's best, it doesn't mean that you are man's best. Many times, God's choice conflicts with man's choice. Many times, what people call God, God calls evil. But when it comes to His kingdom agenda, God's Word holds the upper hand. So, believe in who God says you are, not who man says you are.

David

> Saul said to David, "Here is my older daughter Merab. I will give her to you in marriage; only serve me bravely and fight the battles of the LORD." For Saul said to himself, "I will not raise a hand against him. Let the Philistines do that!" But David said to Saul, "Who am I, and what is my family or my clan in Israel, that I should become the king's son-in-law?" ¹⁹ So when the time came for Merab, Saul's daughter, to be given to David, she was given in marriage to Adriel of Meholah. (1 Samuel 18:17-19 NIV)

In 1 Samuel 18:17, King Saul presents his older daughter, Merab, to David as his wife, and in verse eighteen, David responds, "Who am I, and what is my family or my clan in Israel, that I should become the King's son-in-law?"

David's family background caused his inferiority complex. He did the dirty jobs in his family. He tended to the sheep. His own father had forgotten to introduce him to Prophet Samuel in 1 Samuel 16:6-8. David was introduced last only after the prophet asked his father if he had any other children. That must have affected David. Even after he was anointed by Samuel and chosen by God, he still doubted himself. Even after he defeated Goliath, he still doubted himself. Even after he found favor with the King, he still doubted himself.

In 1 Samuel 18:19, we read the devastating effects of David's inferiority complex. It says, "So when the time came for Merab, Saul's daughter, to be given to David, she was given in marriage to Adriel of Meholah." Sometimes, we hold on to an inferiority complex, and we end up losing the blessings that God had in store for us because we don't see ourselves as worthy.

David is a classic example of someone who battled with an inferiority complex all his life. He was a man after God's own heart, but he needed the approval of all sorts of women to make him feel like a man. If David lived today, and he was my personal friend, I would advise counseling because his inferiority complex ran deep.

Everyone called of God feels unworthy at one point because our God is worthy and holy. So, I want to attribute David's inferiority complex to his upbringing. He was never inside his father's house but always in the bush.

Becoming the King's son-in-law was unimaginable to a boy who had spent most of his time in the bush. And physically, that is true, but spiritually, that is not who David was. He was more than just a son-in-law to the King—there was a King embedded in him. I want every pastor's wife to realize David overcame the fact that he was just a son-in-law. You will overcome the inferiority complex and wear the crown that God has placed on your head in very comfortable shoes. Go on and run the race!

Identifying the Signs

After examining Jeremiah, Gideon, Moses, and David, which of their struggles can you most relate to? Perhaps it's Moses' physical impediment or David's struggle with his family background? Each of them had differing signs of an inferiority complex in their lives. Can you identify if you have any of the signs in the following list and, if so, what caused them?

- You're a perfectionist because you strive to prove you are as good or better than others.

- You want to be perceived as competent because you don't want to be rejected.
- You're most comfortable fading into the background because you're afraid of failing, rejection, or timid because you lack confidence.
- You're very sensitive to criticism.
- You tend to find faults in others.
- You only feel good about yourself when you think you're doing better than others.
- You don't believe it when people compliment you.
- You're quick to assume the worst.
- You feel the need to over-compensate.

Do any of these signs describe you? If so, can you trace how it started?

Even if you have all the signs, you are not irredeemable. If you feel like you need help, get help from a trained Christian counselor. In the meantime, give this burden to the Almighty. The Bible says, "Come to me, all who labor and are heavy laden and I will give you rest. Take my yoke upon you, and learn from me, for I am gentle and lowly in heart, and you will find rest for your souls. For my yoke is easy and my burden is light" (Matthew 11:28-30 NKJV).

Find rest in Him who knows you better than you know yourself. Do not be afraid of the call of God because of an inferiority complex. Allow God to work within you as He uses you. Allow Him to turn that weakness into strength. Remember, you are who God says you are.

More Solutions: Renew Your Mind to Who God Says You Are

To overcome an inferiority complex, it is crucial to uproot the devil's lies and renew your mind with who the Word of God says you are. The Word of God, not your background, physical stature, or eloquence, dictates who you are.

A Royal Priest

> He has made us a Kingdom of priests for God his Father. All glory and power to him forever and ever! Amen. (Revelation 1:6 NLT)
>
> But you are a chosen people, a royal priesthood, a holy nation, God's special possession, that you may declare the praises of him who called you out of darkness into his wonderful light. (1 Peter 2:9 NIV)

I don't know what people call you, but God calls you His priest—His minister. People in the church may be calling you names, but the Word of God has the final say. People don't have the final say about you—God has the final say. Remember, you are a priest—period. Anything contrary doesn't count. Everything else doesn't matter. So, it's better for you as a pastor's wife to focus on who God is saying you are, not what people are saying. Don't allow any other description of you to weigh you down. God has already identified you through His Word, and that's the best identity. Nothing beats that!

You are a "god" woman.

> I said, "You *are* gods, And all of you *are* children of the Most High. (Psalms 82:6 NKJV)

> So the LORD said to Moses: "See, I have made you *as* God to Pharaoh, and Aaron your brother shall be your prophet. (Exodus 7:1 NKJV)

God identifies you as a god (Elohim, a mighty one), so you are more than a pastor's wife. If God calls you a god, you can govern that pastor's wife's office. You're good enough to govern it, according to your identification in the Scriptures.

When we look at Exodus 7:1, remember how Moses was undermining himself by focusing on his speech impediment. God still identified him as a "God" to pharaoh. That's God with a capital G.

What you're scared of as a pastor's wife, God has made you a god over. God has made you a god over what you're trying to run away from. And from this day, I'd like you to know that just like Moses, before God positioned you, He made you a God over that office.

The God of Moses is the same God that appointed you. So quit looking down on yourself and look at yourself as a woman of authority and power. See yourself as a woman who determines what happens and what should happen next because a god has the capability to determine what can happen next. You permit what comes in and what goes out. You either stop or move things. The authority is in your hands. You are not who you thought you were because of your impediment. And now that you have been identified as a god, that so-called impediment is under your feet. It cannot stop you. It cannot block you. It cannot hinder you.

> And in Lystra a certain man without strength in his feet was sitting, a cripple from his mother's womb, who had never walked. [9] *This* man heard Paul speaking. Paul, observing him intently and seeing that he had faith to be

healed, [10] said with a loud voice, "Stand up straight on your feet!" And he leaped and walked. [11] Now when the people saw what Paul had done, they raised their voices, saying in the Lycaonian *language,* "The gods have come down to us in the likeness of men!" (Acts 14:8-11 NKJV)

The Lycaonians said, "The gods have come down to us in the likeness of men!" This still upholds the Scripture that says we are gods. When God wants to do something in the earth, He uses men and women. We are the vessels that God uses. As much as some people are waiting for angels, God is prepared to move through men and women. And one of those people that God is coming down through is you, the pastor's wife. So, open yourself up and yield to the Holy Spirit because God wants to move through you to touch the lives of many.

You were created for great things, signs, and wonders.

> Here am I and the children whom the LORD has given me! *We* are for signs and wonders in Israel From the LORD of hosts, Who dwells in Mount Zion. (Isaiah 8:18 NKJV)

You were formed for great things; this is one of the Scriptures you can fight back with when the spirit of inferiority is creeping on you. Remind the devil that you are made for signs and wonders, not depression and oppression.

You carry the presence of God.

> And I heard a loud voice from heaven saying, "Behold, the tabernacle of God *is* with men, and He will dwell with them, and they shall be His people. God Himself will be with them *and be* their God. (Revelation 21:3 NKJV)

The presence of God is with men. I want every pastor's wife to remember that you are His tabernacle. You are carrying His presence, so minister to the people from that office—from His presence. You can execute the responsibilities of the pastor's wife's office because His presence is with you.

In the next section, we discuss those responsibilities in greater detail and provide guidance for fulfilling them.

SECTION TWO: RESPONSIBILITIES OF EVERY PASTOR'S WIFE

Each pastor's wife has her own unique giftings and capabilities, but each pastor's wife shares two responsibilities—intercession and mothering. She may or may not have biological children, but as a pastor's wife, she is a mother in Zion, and that is an office. She must intercede, as Christ calls all New Testament believers to do (Ephesians 6:12-18), and she must be an example other women can follow. This section addresses the key responsibilities of intercession and motherhood.

Chapter 5: Intercession: It Matters if You Pray

"Likewise the Spirit also helps in our weaknesses. For we do not know what we should pray for as we ought, but the Spirit Himself makes intercession for us with groanings which cannot be uttered." – Paul in Romans 8:26 NKJV

The Holy Spirit is a helper (John 14:16 NKJV); that is His role in believers' lives. As a helper, He does various things, including prayer. Similarly, as a pastor's wife, your marital assignment is to be a God-given helper to your husband. Your position in your husband's life is similar to the ministry of the Holy Spirit. If the Holy Spirit, who is a helper, prays and makes intercession, then wives, who are also helpers, should pray and make intercession for their husbands.

As a helper, the Holy Spirit's assignment and mission include:

1. *Intercession:* Romans 8:26 says the Holy Spirit prays. He makes intercession and helps us to pray when we don't know what to say. As part of His role as a helper, the Holy Spirit is an intercessor. So, you ought to intercede for your husband, especially when he doesn't know what to do.

2. ***Guidance into truth:*** He guides believers into truth through spiritual hearing. John 16:13 says, "However, when He, the Spirit of truth, has come, He will guide you into all truth; for He will not speak on His own authority, but whatever He *hears* He will speak" (NKJV, italics added). Pastor's wives should also hear from God and declare what they hear to their husbands. But how will you hear from God if you're not in the place of prayer frequently? Pastor's wife, if you don't pray, you will mislead your man of God.
3. ***Guidance into the future through spiritual sight:*** John 16:13 says, "He [Holy Spirit] will *shew you* things to come" (KJV, brackets and italics added). Through prayer, wives gain insight from the Holy Spirit to help their husbands avoid errors and future pitfalls.

Jesus also instructs us to pray. He spoke a parable to His disciples about prayer, admonishing them to always pray and not faint. He said:

> "There was in a certain city a judge who did not fear God nor regard man. 3 Now there was a widow in that city; and she came to him, saying, 'Get justice for me from my adversary.' 4 And he would not for a while; but afterward he said within himself, 'Though I do not fear God nor regard man, 5 yet because this widow troubles me I will avenge her, lest by her continual coming she weary me.' " 6 Then the Lord said, "Hear what the unjust judge said. 7 And shall God not avenge His own elect who cry out day and night to Him, though He bears long with them? 8 I tell you that He will avenge them speedily. Nevertheless, when the Son of Man comes, will He really find faith on the earth?" (Luke 18:2-8 NKJV)

Intercession: The Ministry of All Pastors' Wives

All men everywhere—no matter their calling or vocation—should pray. Therefore, every pastor's wife should pray and make intercession for her husband, children, and church. There are no excuses—and no exceptions. James 5:16 says, ". . . pray for each other . . . The earnest prayer of a righteous person has great power and produces wonderful results" (NLT). I want you to understand that prayer and intercession are duties of your office. So, let's understand what intercession is.

What is intercession?

Intercession is praying on behalf of another. An intercessor petitions God and makes requests on their behalf but also stands between Satan's agenda for them and God's will for their life. They veto Satan's plans and enforce the will of God for a person's life, a nation, family, church, leader, etc., by taking authority in prayer.

There is a difference between a prayer warrior and an intercessor. Warriors may pray once about a matter, but intercessors pray for someone until they become a praise in the earth. They are a watchman committed to their post. They do not stop praying until the mission is accomplished fully—not halfway.

Prayer warriors might pray from the emotional realm instead of the God realm. They may be excited initially or loud in church but never take the matter up again. Prayer warriors may not be consistent, but an intercessor prays consistently.

Intercessors pray the prayers of God (the heart and mind of God)—not their own prayers. They don't pray for their will but God's will to be done. They carry God's burden and agenda over nations, territories, regions, homes, and marriages. They are not self-seeking but have a passion for God's Kingdom to come on Earth as it is in heaven.

They are vetted by God Himself to stand in the gap on behalf of others. So, every pastor's wife is vetted by God to handle the job of being an intercessor for their husband—that includes you. God wants you and every other pastor's wife to realize how much power is at your disposal through prayer. Remember, fights and arguments in the home or ministry change nothing, but prayer does.

Here are some important keys to help you fulfill your assignment to pray for your husband.

Covenant gives you privileges in prayer.

Pastor's wife, you are your husband's helper with a position comparable to the Holy Spirit. So be confident that God listens to you first when you pray for your husband-pastor, the vision holder of the church. Being in covenant with him gives you preeminence before God in intercession for him, unlike intercessors and church workers in the congregation.

Church intercessors who assure your husband they will pray for him can only get so far. For instance, God told Abraham to listen to his wife, Sarah, not Hagar, because Sarah was in covenant (Genesis 21:12). Moreover, as much as Hagar also cried out to God and even more than the lad, God did not respond to her. He heard the voice of the lad—not Hagar—because he was the child of Abraham, who was in covenant (Genesis 21:17). Indeed, covenant gives you privileges in prayer.

As a helper, your husband's weaknesses are your prayer assignment.

The Bible says the Holy Spirit helps in our infirmities, which mean weaknesses. You are also a helper assigned to pray for your husband's weaknesses. God entrusted you with him so you can help him become who God has called him to be. But remember, you're also a mortal man, so how can you help another mortal man?

By accessing the supernatural power of God through prayer, you can help your husband's weaknesses. For example, a man went to cheat on his wife. But because of the prayers of the wife, when he got there, he and the other woman got into a very bad fight, and all their pre-planned sex could not happen.

I beseech every pastor's wife, by the mercies of God, to choose prayer over controlling a man and having cheap fights. You can place your husband on a remote control called prayer. Engage in prayer and take control of him spiritually, not physically. Remember, the spirit realm is more powerful and dominant than the natural or physical realm. Thus, what you do in the spirit realm will determine the outcome or results in the physical realm. (2 Corinthians 4:18)

You are your husband's Aaron and Hur (Exodus 17:12-14).

Aaron and Hur upheld Moses' arms until Israel gained victory. Once you stop upholding your husband in prayer, victory will diminish. So, arise and pray him into his destiny, greatness, and God's glory.

You are your husband's Deborah, called to lead him to victory like Deborah led Barak to divine fulfillment and victory (Judges 4:8-10). Your advice must be one of a kind to advance him into God's purpose for his life and fulfilling God's call on his life. Your counsel should never lead him in the opposite direction of God's purpose and will for his life.

There are certain things a man of God will never achieve until you, his God-ordained spouse, step into that boat with him and declare, "We can make it" or "Let's go!" Men's cheers and applause are encouraging, but there is nothing more encouraging than your spouse cheering you on. Men can hail you in ministry, but if your family doesn't hail you, it doesn't mean much.

God created a ministry called the Garden of Eden, and the first member of that ministry was Eve. When Eve failed, Adam failed. So, the success of many men's ministries is very dependent on their wives or who they marry.

Add fasting to your prayers for your husband.

> Then Esther sent this reply to Mordecai: [16] "Go, gather together all the Jews who are in Susa, and fast for me. Do not eat or drink for three days, night or day. I and my attendants will fast as you do. When this is done, I will go to the king, even though it is against the law. And if I perish, I perish." (Esther 4:15-16 NIV)

Esther had an assignment to use her God-given favor to keep the king from making the grievous mistake of alienating the Jews. This would have caused God to curse the king, but because God knew he was being wrongly influenced, He sent Esther to help the king so that he would not offend God. Esther fulfilled her assignment through fasting and prayer.

It takes prayer to help a man of God because divine wisdom is deposited in a man, home, and ministry through prayer. Esther was beautiful, but beauty alone could not change the heart of the king and cause him to spare her when she violated government protocol and went into his court unannounced. She didn't come to the kingdom only because she was beautiful or by coincidence.

Prayer will give you access to a man's heart—even a king. Proverbs 21:1 says, "The king's heart *is* in the hand of the LORD, *Like* the rivers of water; He turns it wherever He wishes" (NKJV). It was through prayer and fasting that Esther gained great influence with her husband. After engaging in intense prayer, the king told her she could ask for whatever she wanted, up to half of his kingdom (Esther 5:4).

It was prayer that helped Esther understand the will of God; prayer brings illumination. She got the bigger picture that she was there, in the king's court, for a divine agenda. God had a plan to save the nation, and because she fasted and prayed, she was able to carry out that assignment.

Fasting will also empower you, but before you embark on your journey of fasting, consider Isaiah 58:

> 'Why have we fasted,' they say, 'and you have not seen it? Why have we humbled ourselves, and you have not noticed?' "Yet on the day of your fasting, you do as you please and exploit all your workers. [4] Your fasting ends in quarreling and strife, and in striking each other with wicked fists. You cannot fast as you do today and expect your voice to be heard on high. [5] Is this the kind of fast I have chosen, only a day for people to humble themselves? Is it only for bowing one's head like a reed and for lying in sackcloth and ashes? Is that what you call a fast, a day acceptable to the LORD? [6] "Is not this the kind of fasting I have chosen: to loose the chains of injustice and untie the cords of the yoke, to set the oppressed free and break every yoke? [7] Is it not to share your food with the hungry and to provide the poor wanderer with shelter—when you see the naked, to clothe them, and not to turn away from your own flesh and blood? [8] Then your light will break forth like the dawn, and your healing will quickly appear;

then your righteousness will go before you, and the glory of the LORD will be your rear guard. ⁹ Then you will call, and the LORD will answer; you will cry for help, and he will say: Here am I. (Isaiah 58:3-9 NIV)

There is an acceptable and unacceptable way to fast. When you fast, God wants you to have the right attitude, put away strife, and bless others. When you do, He promises that your light will shine forth, you will be healed, His glory on your life will increase, He will answer when you cry to Him, and He will be with you.

There are also several other benefits of fasting to consider.
- It was through fasting that Daniel was able to win spiritual warfare and overcome the principality of Persia (Daniel 10).
- Fasting will enable you to see the will of God manifest. Prophet Anna fasted until she saw the face of Jesus on the earth (Luke 2:37-39). So fasting quickens divine manifestations.
- It will help you subdue sin because the flesh becomes weaker, which gives you more power to resist the desires of the flesh. People who fast are better positioned to fulfill the will of God or walk in the will of God because their spirits are stronger than their flesh.
- Fasting also helps you receive direction and guidance from God. Acts 13:2 says, "As they ministered to the Lord and fasted, the Holy Spirit said, 'Now separate to Me Barnabas and Saul for the work to which I have called them'" (NKJV). If they hadn't fasted, they wouldn't have gotten direction from God.

Fasting also intensifies the power of God in your prayers (Mark 9:39) and helps prepare you for ministry (Luke 4:14). For example, when I was in high school, God spoke to a classmate to tell me to fast for two days. They told me God wanted to deposit something in my life, but I had to consecrate myself through fasting. As a teenager, I ate and drank nothing for two days. It did not come easy, but I endured and prayed through the two days. When my classmates went to eat breakfast and dinner, I went to pray. As they were busy feasting, I was busy praying.

On the last day of the fast, I received a powerful encounter and visitation. A very strong presence of God came and blew on me. I felt like paper in the air. I could see waves of glory in this wind. Behind me was a football field, but to my surprise, no one saw what was happening to me. The girl next to me did not touch me while we were praying. And from that experience and visitation, if I touched anyone or looked them straight in the eye, they were being slain. Even if I was just touching their hand, people were just falling under the power. That power continued to be upon my life—even when I went back to my father's house.

One day, I was praying with the kids in the servants' quarters. As I sang hallelujah, they lifted up their hands, and their hands began to shake intensely. The power of God continued to intensify until they were all on the ground. Just about the same time, my mother walked out of the main house. When she saw it, she began to laugh. She thought I had pushed the kids. She challenged me to hold the prayer meeting inside the main house the following day if what had happened was really God. She made sure to be there.

I began the prayer meeting the next day in the house by worshipping and singing hallelujah. The presence of God began to descend again, and the hands of these same kids began to shake uncontrollably. I was shaking too, but I continued to worship.

After a few minutes, I looked around, and my mother was no longer sitting in her chair, so I wondered where she had gone or what happened. She did not say anything to me, but I really wanted to find out why she left. However, as an African child, there are some questions you cannot ask your parents.

The following day, she was going to a wedding and left a command. "You will not pray in my house. I don't understand what is on you. Yesterday, I began to shake and had to run out of the living room." That is when I learned that she ran out because the power of God was touching her, and she wanted to avoid the embarrassment because she thought I was making it up.

This kind of power and anointing was downloaded on me through fasting. That is why I highly urge every pastor's wife to fast. Fasting will give you access to God's power and glory. Every pastor's wife who does not want to be an ordinary pastor's wife must wield power through prayer and fasting. One of the most important people I trusted in the ministry told me, "Just like the Father, Son, and Holy Spirit are a trinity, if you want to operate in certain dimensions in God, the recipe is prayer, fasting, and giving!" (Matthew 6).

Allow me to submit to you that a pastor's wife who does not fast and pray cannot achieve divine purpose or help guide her husband into the will and purpose of God. She will never access certain dimensions of God or find out what's on the mind of Christ. She will become the kind of pastor's wife who focuses only on what her husband can give her and thinks progress in ministry is only financial and material multiplication and increase. This is not the mark when it comes to ministry. We achieve our mark before God when the man of God fulfills what God called him to do; that is what God calls success—when the man of God is walking in the right path.

There are some pastor's wives whose prayerlessness and focus on materialism led their husbands into error. For example, if the pastor travels a lot, they nag him about when they will travel too.

They want to change cars and homes. They complain that their shoes have grown old, and they want new clothes when they are not needed.

We don't travel to show off; we travel for divine assignment. This constant nagging can cause a man of God to err, and it comes from a carnal place, not from a place of prayer or seeking God. So, we have to be careful that our material cravings and demands don't cause the man of God to err because sometimes destinies are unretrievable. Prayerlessness can lead to errors that close doors that apologies cannot reopen.

Prayerlessness subverts our Kingdom responsibility.

Prayer is a lifeline. Prayerlessness is a lost lifeline. Through prayer, the will of God is enforced, and the will of the enemy is destroyed.

If a pastor's wife fails to execute the will of God after she gets into her marriage or in the case of Queen Esther, the palace, she can be replaced. We can see this in Esther 4:14, where Mordecai warns Esther that if she does not arise to save her Jewish heritage, deliverance for the Jews would come from somewhere else, and she and her father's house would perish. She was in the palace or the marriage "for such a time as this" to execute a critical divine agenda to save the Jews. Failure to do so would cause her to lose not only her life but also her position as queen—just like her predecessor, Vashti.

The pastor's wife's office is not to be taken for granted or lightly. It's serious kingdom business. Should you fail at your assignment, God can find someone else. Like David and Saul's situation, He can qualify the disqualified. When Saul failed to obey God, He replaced him with David, who was a mere shepherd and more passionate about pleasing Him than having the throne. Some women enjoy the throne, but they don't want the responsibility that comes with sitting on it. If you must enjoy the throne, execute the responsibility that comes with it.

In the next chapter, we discuss the motherhood responsibility of a pastor's wife.

Chapter 6: Nurturing: The Art of Spiritual Motherhood

"And I will bless her [Sarah] and give thee a son also of her: yea, I will bless her, and she shall be a mother of nations; kings of people shall be of her." — God speaking to Abraham in Genesis 17:16b KJV, brackets added

As Sarah was a mother of nations, every pastor's wife is a mother in Zion. This is not an old-school mindset; it's a reality. No matter her age, every pastor's wife is a covenant co-heir with her husband, worthy of the congregation's respect. (We will address why the congregation must respect her in more detail later in the chapter.) The pastor's wife must not relinquish her responsibility to other women in the church—even the older women or those who have been in ministry longer than her.

As a mother, the pastor's wife is a nurturer, womb carrier, and female parent. There is a certain care only a mother can give to her children, lovingly providing nourishment that comes only from her body. She carries a womb and should avail herself to the womb of prayer, giving birth to the seed of vision planted in her by the Holy Spirit and aiding in birthing the vision God gave her husband.

She is the female parent of the ministry. Yes, the pastor's wife's office is a mothering office that comes with a responsibility to nurture, advise, and admonish, which are vital aspects of the art of spiritual motherhood.

Nurture, advise, and admonish.

As the female parent, every pastor's wife has souls to nurture. Her individual gifts and unique heavenly calling determine the specific ways she does so in the church (apart from intercession). Still, there are things only she can do that her husband cannot do, and she will have a manner, grace, and touch in doing it that he will never have. It's a mother's office to nurture, correct, and guide with care.

For example, Proverbs 31 is something many people have a misconception about. They think it was written for women. But it was a woman giving her son advice and guidance; it was written by a woman—a mother—for her son, instructing him how to tell the difference between a virtuous woman and a harlot. It was "The utterance which his mother *taught* him" (Proverbs 31:10 NKJV, italics added). His mother was teaching him things pertaining to women.

There are certain secrets mothers unleash to their sons that fathers cannot because it takes a woman to know a woman. Even kings, in this case, King Lemuel, were advised by their mothers. She was telling him the dos and don'ts of life. She was preparing him for what he should be careful with; things like women, intoxicating drinks, and how to identify a virtuous woman. She was teaching him how to preserve his strength for rulership. She says, "Do not spend your strength on women, your vigor on those who ruin kings" (Proverbs 31:3 NIV).

In Proverbs 31:10, she asks, "Who can find a virtuous woman?" This is simply a forecast for King Lemuel to know that it's a search and takes effort to find a virtuous woman. She doesn't just fall into your lap. No, you must take careful consideration when choosing a wife. She is someone with whom you'll spend the rest of your life.

So, the king's mother lays down the characteristics of a virtuous woman so her son can look out for that character in his search. This means not every woman is a virtuous one. Not every woman is a mother. There's a difference between a mother and a surrogate.

Pastor's wife, don't be a surrogate.

The true art of motherhood is bringing forth and nurturing what you have delivered into its destiny. Surrogates don't nurture what they bring forth. After delivery, they give up their motherhood responsibilities and walk away.

There's a lot of spiritual death in ministry because mothers are not nurturing what they have brought forth. After being born again through the spiritual labor and delivery called regeneration, many believers have no one to breastfeed them and nurture them in the things of God. So, they die. Even in the natural, very few newborns make it through infancy without a mother (or a mother-like person) to care for them.

Even worse, in the present-day church, some spiritual children are dying because the mother-child roles have been reversed. Mothers are not feeding their children spiritually; they are keeping everything for themselves and becoming spiritually obese. They are too fat spiritually and have no successors because their ministries focus only on themselves.

They don't care to raise up their children because they are focused on money and who is giving the biggest tithe. This causes them to ignore the true spiritual children who could succeed them in ministry because it is not about what they give as a mother but what they receive. Unfortunately, people can give huge tithes yet still not carry the seed of greatness or holiness in them.

May you not be among the women who abandon their babies when they need their mother the most, in Jesus' name. Instead, may your children be comforted and calmed in your care. Psalm 131:2 says, "Surely I have calmed and quieted my soul, Like a weaned child with his mother; Like a weaned child *is* my soul within me" (NKJV). Are your children comforted and quieted in your arms? Isaiah 66:13 also says, "As a mother comforts her child, so will I comfort you; and you will be comforted over Jerusalem" (NIV).

May you fight for your children like Jochebed, Moses' mother. Exodus 2:3 shows that she fought for his destiny. She was determined that her child would not die like the sons of other Hebrew women. So, she hid him and placed him in the river where Pharoah's daughter later found him.

Jochebed recognized that her son was a blessing. Yes, to be a mother is not a right but a privilege and a blessing from God. Psalm 127:3 says, "Children are a heritage from the LORD, offspring a reward from him" (NIV). Motherhood is an honor, and pastors' wives must respect that office by carrying out the duties that come with it. Their husbands and congregation members should also ensure they are respected.

The mothering office must be respected—by all.

However great someone is, they would never exist without a mother. However anointed or gifted, everyone has a mother and came through the channel called motherhood. Mothers (pastors' wives) are not consequential; they are essential.

That is why people who are determined to respect the pastor while disrespecting the pastor's wife are misplaced. You have people who claim the pastor as their father but openly declare, "The wife is not my mother." They honor the pastor as a father but not the wife as a mother. Every person on Earth has a mother, and so does every ministry and local congregation. The ministry has a womb (Isaiah 49:5), and such people must check themselves.

The Bible says honor your father *and* mother in the Lord—not just your father (Exodus 20:12, Deuteronomy 5:16, Matthew 15:4, Matthew 19:19, Mark 7:10, Mark 10:19, Luke 1:43, Luke 18:20, Ephesians 6:2-3). Every church member should submit themselves to be fathered *and* mothered. Indeed, there are severe consequences when church members are not mothered.

Ironically, female church members often reject the ministry of motherhood because they have problems with female authority or never experience a true example of motherhood in their own lives.

You can identify unmothered women by the negative patterns that follow them.

The way many women in the church conduct themselves reveals whether they had mothers or were motherless.

Some characteristics of unmothered women are:

1. They don't like to be taught because they have grown up teaching themselves everything—literally. Thus, they carry an unteachable spirit. They know better or know more than everyone. They come to the pastor not to be pastored but to tell them what's best. In other

words, they want to instruct the mother in the house because of their know-more attitude.

2. No one corrects them when they make mistakes. They are defensive about everything they do. They never accept any mistakes they make; they always have an excuse for their behavior. They are not submissive. Who corrects you when you err?

3. They deem correction and rebuke as rejection. They only love praises; everything must be good, even if you, the pastor's wife or co-pastor, see things in their life that are out of order. When you take on the mandate to correct them, they see it as you rejecting them. That is a big misconception. We should learn to differentiate between rebuke and rejection. The Lord corrects those whom He loves (Hebrews 12:6). So, the fact that you take the time to correct a church member is a sign of love. Correction must not be deemed as rejection.

4. They compete in the house of God, even with the pastor's wife, the spiritual mother of the house. In God's house, we don't compete: We complete one another. You don't strive to have what your mother has because you are not—and can never be—grace mates with your mother. Mothers carry a different grace than their daughters. You can never be equal to your mother because mothers have built a memorial through years of prayer, and some of you are just getting started. They have a mother's grace, but you have a daughter's grace. The difference should be crystal clear.

5. They don't know their spiritual jurisdiction. They move from one location to another anyway, anyhow. They jump from place to place, from church to church. However, a Deborah must know the place of her jurisdictional authority or calling because that's where they are most effective (Judges 4:5). Deborah dwelt between Ramah and Bethel. Deborahs define their boundaries, but unmothered people don't have boundaries. God has not called you everywhere. Know, discover, and focus on the location of your calling.

Mothers, arise!

Mothers must arise for some principalities to crumble before their children. If you don't arise as a mother, some principalities will govern your generations. Deborah had to rise for Jabin and Sisera to fall (Judges 5:7). Mothers have several responsibilities, roles, and assignments, including to:

- War for their children (Judges 4: 9)
- Direct their children (Judges 4:14)
- Be torchbearers for their children (set the pace; show them the way they should take, direct, scan through the future, and see where their children should and should not go) (Proverbs 6:20-22, Judges 4:14)
- Nurture their children; feed them spiritually and physically (1 Peter 2:2, Proverbs 22:6, Psalm 131:2)
- Encourage and strengthen their children (Isaiah 66:13)
- Protect their children (Moses' mother did the best to protect him from assassination by Pharoah.) (Exodus 2:3)
- Discipline their children (Proverbs 13:24, 23:13-14, 29:17, 19:18)
- Help their children defeat strong enemies (Judges 5:7-9, 24-

27)
- Interpret and download the voice of God in the lives of their children (Luke 1:41-45, 59-60, Proverbs 31:1-31)

This is the motherhood job description. Unfortunately, some church members don't welcome this ministry from their pastor's wife. They don't like discipline, even though it's very important in every child's life.

I have met some children who were not mothered, and the damage is irreparable. They haven't made it far in life. They have not fulfilled their destinies—not because they cannot but because of the absence of a mother who executed the motherhood job description without fear.

Be a nurturer of destinies.

Israel had a destiny but needed a mother to nurture it (Judges 5:7). As great a nation as Israel was, it could not progress without the aspect of spiritual motherhood to preserve, protect, and direct it. Deborah said, "Village life ceased, it ceased in Israel, Until I, Deborah, arose, Arose a mother in Israel" (Judges 5:7 NKJV). Life as they knew it ceased, which means so many people in that generation were stuck, stagnant, unproductive, confused, misplaced, and dead because of the lack of a mother to guide, direct, and protect them. This is also true today. All aspects of society were impacted, including the economy, travel industry, and trade.

A lack of motherhood also affected the spiritual aspect of society. Until Deborah arose, the beloved nation of God also turned to idols. "They chose new gods; Then *there was* war in the gates" (Judges 5:8 NKJV). Mothers must arise to halt idolatry in their bloodlines and keep their children from serving false gods. They must arise to release the next generation to the right path.

If Deborahs don't rise up, potential destiny changers and powerful spiritual warriors, like Jael, who killed Sisera with a tent peg, will not rise up. No one knew Jael's capability until Deborah arose as a mother in her generation. If you don't arise, potential game-changing women in your generation will never realize their potential either. They will die because of laziness and passiveness. Someone needs you to arise!

Don't be passive, and don't give up easily. Destinies are messy, and children make mistakes.

As a pastor's wife, you will mother many under the umbrella of your husband-pastor or other ministry assignments. So, brace yourself because children do make mistakes and are born with many spiritual issues.

As in the natural, some infants are born with complications, and some spiritual children also get born again with issues, spiritual diseases, or challenges. But as the mother of the church, are you going to throw them away because of birth defects? Absolutely not. The way forward is to treat their defects by praying for them, nursing their spiritual wounds, and nurturing them into their destinies.

I will never forget the day one of the children God had instructed me to nurture came to me and revealed a shocking truth. She said she was coming to every service in the church because she was simply looking for an opportunity to sleep with my husband, who happened to be the pastor.

She revealed that the demons that were using her told her that I was aware of her agenda, which was true. God spoke to me about her intentions, but they did not fit the physical look on her face and her attitude toward me. She looked so humble and innocent, but the Spirit told me something different. At some point, I doubted myself, but God confirmed it through another intercessor. They received the same revelation about her during a forty-day fast in church.

So, we began to abort her assignment through prayer and fasting. After an overnight prayer meeting, this lady said she heard the voice of God telling her, "If you don't repent, you're going to die." She thought God was joking, but as we were leaving the overnight meeting, I was talking with an elder at my car. She was asking me the secret of seeing in the spirit. While we were still talking, I received a phone call asking if I was still in the parking lot and not to leave; they were coming back because of an issue. The elder asked me what was going on, and I told her I knew what was going on and who they were bringing. They brought this lady back to the parking lot. She was shaking and could not breathe well.

When the elder saw her, her heart sank, and we kept quiet to hear what she had to say. She was crying intensely and shaking under the power of God. She cried, "Pastor, I'm sorry. You have never done anything to me." After confessing, she said she was leaving the church.

I told her that was not the solution. She had exposed the devil, and he could no longer use her. "All you have to work on is your deliverance," I said. Many pastors' wives thought I was foolish to let her stay in the ministry. They could not believe how I handled the matter. According to them, they would have thrown her out and wanted nothing to do with her. I remember sharing this story at a pastor's wives conference in Dallas, Texas. They had many questions and could not believe how I handled it and moved forward with her.

I want to assure you that every child you have in ministry will not be perfect. However, your responsibility to correct, rebuke, chastise, and nurture them will remain. When I sought God further about this situation, He asked me, "If you delivered a child with special needs, would you throw him or her away?" Of course not.

Today, many children in ministry have special needs. As a pastor's wife, not everyone you're going to nurture will be upright. They will have to get out of certain dark lines into the lines of light. To help them, we must exhibit patience, which is a fruit of the Holy Spirit. We must show maturity, understanding, and the heart of God towards the children we are called to nurture.

I saw no reason to cast this lady out of the church. She was already renouncing the devil, which is victory in the Kingdom. When an agent of Satan turns into an agent of light, the dark kingdom has fallen.

Through patience, this lady has grown, transformed, and is walking in holiness. She was able to marry and is serving in the ministry. She has never repeated or shown any sign of lust towards my husband. She has kept her distance from him because she's aware of where God picked her from.

This is a lesson also; if you discover the devil wants to use you in a certain area, avoid it as much as possible. For example, if the devil wants to tempt you with cigarettes, don't play around with them. You'll be playing with a time bomb.

If I hadn't been patient, this sister wouldn't have transformed. I'm thankful to the Holy Spirit, who gave me the patience and guidance to navigate my way through this. I believe this is what they call nurturing. But for most pastor's wives, this is would have been a no-go area—a "don't touch the dial" situation. I'm not saying a pastor's wife should compromise, but if someone is willing to change, give them a chance. However, if someone is stubborn and continuously seductive, you have the right to drive them away from the ministry because they will become a distraction. For me, the story of this girl is a story of successful nurturing in ministry and a demonstration of the art of motherhood.

In addition to intercession and mothering, the next chapter explores several dos and don't's of the pastor's wife's office to consider.

Chapter 7: Dos and Don'ts for Every Pastor's Wife

"Principles and rules are intended to provide a thinking man with a frame of reference." – Carl von Clausewitz

"Wisdom is knowing what to do next. Skill is knowing how to do it. Virtue is doing it." - Thomas Jefferson

The Oxford Dictionary defines dos and don'ts as rules of behavior. Such rules are connected to principles that provide a frame of reference for applying wisdom in specific situations and issues. There is a common set of situations and issues that affect all pastors' wives and a corresponding set of common dos and don'ts, or rules of behavior, that will keep them from unnecessary drama, protect them and their families' privacy, and help them fulfill their role with grace and wisdom. So, let's discuss a few important dos and don'ts useful to you, the pastor's wife, for wisdom, skill, and virtue.

Do heed the charge to leaders' wives in the book of 1 Timothy.

Paul lists the qualifications of church overseers (senior pastors and bishops), deacons, and wives or female leaders in 1 Timothy 3. He says, "In the same way, the women are to be worthy of respect, not malicious talkers but temperate and trustworthy in everything" (1 Timothy 3:11 NIV). To be a malicious talker is to be a slanderer, and a temperate person is a self-controlled and disciplined person.

So, Paul is saying that a pastor's wife should:

- Live a lifestyle worthy of respect. Others should look at your life and manner of living and respect the way you live for God and represent Him. This includes integrity, being faithful in your marriage and the ministry, and showing respect to others.
- Be a good representative of God as a believer, wife, and ministry leader.
- Be respectful; some people in the congregation will be older than you. As much as you hold the motherhood office, you must deal with them respectfully.
- Never be a malicious talker or slanderer. A pastor's wife must know how to tame her tongue.
- Be temperate, self-controlled, and disciplined. You must not be a drunkard or pursue dishonest gain. You should not display attitudes or explode on your husband or children—especially at church.

Paul is giving the pastor's wife a set of dos and don'ts. The fact that Paul includes wives or female leaders in his list of qualifications means that God takes female leadership seriously and requires the wives of male leaders to be mature and worthy of respect.

Note that Paul focuses on the pastors' wife's character not glamour. If you allow God to work on your character, you will broaden your "Mother wings," allowing God to trust you with more and more influence because He knows you will impart character and virtue. Pastor's wife, your office is important to

God!

Do choose your wardrobe well to represent God well.

We've talked about this in previous chapters. However, the fact that the pastor's wife's wardrobe is a make-or-break issue cannot be overemphasized. You must be an example, especially to the other women in the congregation. And as Paul said in 1 Timothy 3, the way you dress must be worthy of respect. It must reflect modesty and self-control. Remember to dress appropriately for the pulpit even if you are casual, ensuring that you are not revealing your body parts, and your motive is not to draw attention to yourself. Equally important, make it a priority to allow the Holy Spirit to do His "Holy Ghost check" on your wardrobe before you leave the house.

Do depend on the Holy Spirit personally.

It is important to depend on the Holy Spirit for guidance and direction primarily, not your husband. Your husband needs the help of the same Holy Spirit—and your help too. Also, relying on the Holy Spirit gives you visibility in the spirit concerning where the ministry is going, which empowers you to be of assistance to him.

You must be connected to God personally through His Spirit and not depend on others' relationship with Him. You cannot tap into someone else's spiritual Wi-Fi frequency with God and have your own personal prayer altar at the same time. When a pastor's wife doesn't have a prayer life, she becomes very dependent on church intercessors, her husband, or so-called fiery ministers in the church, which is very dangerous.

Depending on others is like tapping into someone else's public Wi-Fi network. But if that network acquires a virus or hackers, you will automatically acquire them too, and it will affect your vision. Because of your position, if you catch a virus, your husband and the whole church will catch it, which will lead to the destruction of the ministry.

While the ministry is interdependent and needs intercessors, there are certain things you must hear from God for yourself. If you have an active prayer altar, others' input and counsel will be confirmation of what God has already told you. You will avoid misdirection.

Remember, the intercessors are not the vision bearers. You are the co-vision bearer, and you are in charge of receiving divine direction from God. He didn't give them the GPS or navigation system for ministry directions. It is in yours and your husband's hands; you're the co-driver; you're the only one God is depending on to take the driver's seat if something happens to the main driver, your husband.

That's why you have a seat different from everyone else in the ministry. If the vision bearer is sleeping, God is depending on you to shift positions. If he must take a break, rest, or needs a sabbatical, God is depending on you to drive the vision forward. It's very important that you are alert and sober so you can execute the assignment and vision effectively. For example, when Moses's time was over, Joshua had to take the driver's seat. Because he was always there, even when others departed from the tabernacle, he was ready to shift gears without missing a beat:

> "So the LORD spoke to Moses face to face, as a man speaks to his friend. And he would return to the camp, but his servant Joshua the son of Nun, a young man, did not depart from the tabernacle" (Exodus 33:11 NKJV).

Joshua was ready to drive the vision forward in Moses' absence because he stayed connected to God personally. No wonder he was qualified. He was there to observe God's interactions with Moses. He learned how Moses entered God's presence and carefully observed to learn and equip himself.

In the same manner, every pastor's wife ought to tarry in God's presence, even when her husband, who is the vision bearer of the ministry, is not there. I imagine that if Joshua had not spent time in God's presence, he would not have been ready to drive the vision forward. Likewise, spending time in God's presence equips you to drive the vision without fear, or timidity when something happens to the vision bearer.

I have noticed that some pastors' wives cannot even briefly exhort the congregation; they are bankrupt of Scripture, wisdom, and oil because they never spend time in God's presence. Yet, they have time to spend in the shopping malls to get the latest handbag or perfume. This is just a reminder; God is not looking at your handbag or perfume to determine whether to hand the baton to you. He's looking for spiritual substance, passion, and fervency — the fire on your altar — to qualify you to drive a vision forward. So, fix your mindset to focus on things above more than things on Earth. Be determined to connect with the Holy Spirit and depend on Him personally.

Do ask the Holy Spirit to help you choose your inner circle very wisely.

There are many pastors' wives who go about the congregation naively, thinking everyone is for them, attempting to bring everyone close them, and sharing their personal business with many congregation members. This is dangerous because familiarity breeds contempt.

You have to safeguard your family and who knows intimate details about them because you and your family will suffer spiritual attacks that none of the congregation members ever will. The Bible says ". . . smite the shepherd, and the sheep of the flock shall be scattered abroad" (Matthew 26:31 KJV). That means you and your family are the target when the enemy wants to attack the congregation.

You cannot surround yourself with people with spiritual openings like gossip, backbiting, rumor mongering, and other sins the enemy and his demons can use to get to you. You must choose your inner circle wisely, which includes who you share your personal information with, let visit your home, and pray with because there is much at stake.

This is not discriminatory; this is wisdom for the safety and protection of your life, family, and the ministry. Even Jesus had an inner circle among the twelve disciples. There were three, Peter, James, and John, to whom He revealed Himself more intimately than the remaining nine. They were the ones who saw His glorified state on the mount of transfiguration (Matthew 17:1-8). Jesus' example shows us that your inner circle is a very significant determining factor in life.

Thankfully, there are people you can immediately eliminate from your inner circle. Anyone who is competing with you for power or in any aspect of the ministry does merit seeing the intimate details of your personal life. For example, if your inner circle has gossipers, traitors, or betrayers they will open the door for the devil to attack you. Take care that you don't allow anyone with any of these three spirits into your inner circle:

1. The spirit of Judas Iscariot:

> Then one of the twelve, called Judas Iscariot, went to the chief priests ¹⁵ and said, "What are you willing to give me if I deliver Him to you?" And they counted out to him thirty pieces of silver. ¹⁶ So from that time he sought opportunity to betray Him. (Matthew 26:14-16 NKJV)

Discern those in the ministry who are with you for greed and personal gain. They are dishonest with money. They are thieves who will conspire with those who are against you for a mere thirty pieces of silver. They continue to be with you—not because they are faithful and love you—rather, because they are waiting for an opportunity to partner with devil to betray you for gain.

They serve as Satan's open door to enter and attack you. "As soon as Judas took the bread, Satan entered into him. So, Jesus told him, "What you are about to do, do quickly" (John 13:27 NIV). Judas was an open door that Satan entered.

2. The spirit of Absalom:

Absalom was a conspirer, fueled by anger, desire for revenge, and lust for power. He orchestrated his half-brother Amnon's murder, two years after Amnon raped his sister, Tamar. He kept his plot secret, speaking neither good nor bad to Amnon for two years (2 Samuel 13:22). However, at an opportune time, he convinced his father, David, to let Amnon go on a trip with him and had his men kill Amnon once he was merry with wine and partying (2 Samuel 13:29-32). To avoid David's wrath, Absalom fled to Talmi in the land of Geshur for three years.

After three years, Joab, David's general, saw that David missed Absalom and arranged for him to return to Israel. Still, the king refused to see him. For this, Absalom burned Joab's field—the same Joab who convinced his father, David, to let him return to Israel.

Absalom was like a child throwing a temper tantrum when they don't get their way. People with this spirit are full of selfishness and selfish ambition and will sabotage anyone who gets in the way of what they want. Absalom even swayed the hearts of the people of Israel to sabotage his own father and take the throne. He had the beauty and charm to pull it off. The Scripture says, "Absalom was praised as the most handsome man in all Israel. He was flawless from head to foot" (2 Samuel 14:25 NLT). This is the Absalom spirit.

It is a self-seeking, sabotaging spirit that works through gifted and favored sons and daughters you once showed mercy. Still, they turn on you because their lust for power drives them to take what you have. They don't respect your motherhood; they are bold enough to "come for you" and attempt to take your position and all that you have.

3. The spirit of Athaliah:

Athaliah was the granddaughter of King Omri and the daughter of Ahab and Jezebel (2 Kings 8:26, 1 Kings 16:30). She was married to Jehoram, King of Judah, and their son, Ahaziah, became king of Judah. Ahaziah continued in the ways of Ahab and Jezebel, doing evil in God's sight.

> Ahaziah was twenty-two years old when he became king, and he reigned in Jerusalem one year. His mother's name was Athaliah, a granddaughter of Omri king of Israel. [27] He followed the ways of the house of Ahab and did evil in the eyes of the LORD, as the house of Ahab had done, for he was related by marriage to Ahab's family. (2 Kings 8:26-27 NIV)

Ahaziah's reign was short-lived. He died when Jehu fulfilled prophesy by destroying all Ahab's sons and remaining descendants (2 Kings 11). That's when we see Athaliah's true colors. In response to her son's death, she murders all the members of the royal house, killing off all legitimate heirs to the throne so she can reign—she murders her own grandsons. 2 Kings 11:1 says, "When Athaliah the mother of Ahaziah saw that her son was dead, she arose and destroyed all the royal heirs" (NKJV).

At least Athaliah thought she destroyed them all. She did not know that Ahaziah's sister (her daughter) escaped with Ahaziah's son (her grandson), Joash, and hid him.

> But Jehosheba, the daughter of King Joram, sister of Ahaziah, took Joash the son of Ahaziah, and stole him away from among the king's sons *who were* being murdered; and they hid him and his nurse in the bedroom, from Athaliah, so that he was not killed. ³ So he was hidden with her in the house of the LORD for six years, while Athaliah reigned over the land. (2 Kings 11:1-3 NKJV)

After Athaliah reigns seven years, the priests muster courage to ensure Joash is rightfully installed as king and Athaliah is executed.

> And the priest gave the captains of hundreds the spears and shields which *had belonged* to King David, that were in the temple of the LORD. ¹¹ Then the escorts stood, every man with his weapons in his hand, all around the king, from the right side of the temple to the left side of the temple, by the altar and the house. ¹² And he brought out the king's son, put the crown on him, and *gave him* the Testimony; they made him king and anointed him, and they clapped their hands and said, "Long live the king!" (2 Kings 11:10-12 NKJV)

This spirit does want to see the proper order established. She did not want anyone from the line of David to rule but used murder and witchcraft to sacrifice her own grandsons and usurp the throne. This spirit is the daughter of the Jezebel spirit. Protect yourself and your children—don't let anyone who has a rebellious, murderous, usurping spirit into your inner circle.

Do choose your prayer partners wisely.

Related to choosing your inner circle wisely is choosing your prayer partners wisely. The enemy seeks to attack you and your family first because you are leaders. You cannot pray with everybody because some don't have the capacity to handle or address what you'll be confronted with; they're not built for it. So, you must identify your prayer partners wisely. They must be people who:

- Are spiritually mature
- Do not turn back in the day of battle
- Don't break ranks (Joel 2:7-8)

They should not be novices because when the Spirit says certain things they will be offended or unable to handle certain information. As a result, they may hinder you from entering higher dimensions and realms of the spirit. Or they may misinterpret some God-given messages and revelations that come during your prayer times.

My husband and I used to pray with a couple and did not realize they were very immature. There was an occasion when the Lord instructed us to pray a certain prayer, but they were unwilling to follow the instructions. They were unwilling to pray certain prayer points because, to them, it felt like we were attacking a human being. There are times in prayer when God will tell you to draw the sword. When you do, some people will feel like you're trying to kill someone. That ridiculous interpretation showed their spiritual inadequacy to handle what we were confronting.

To pray in one accord with someone, you must have the same spirit and heart. If God is saying wage war and they feel like you should pray for mercy, there's a lack of agreement; you are not in one accord. It's important that you're in sync with your prayer partners so choose them wisely and be bold enough to make changes if needed.

Don't be timid.

"For the Spirit God gave us does not make us timid, but gives us power, love and self-discipline" (2 Timothy 1:7 NIV). Timidity is not given by God. It is the devil's gift.

Precious lives are in your hands—namely your own, your husband's, your children's (if applicable), and congregation members'. You can't afford to let others, or anything intimidate you—not even tradition and religion. Jesus dealt with religious people more harshly, calling them a brood of vipers (Matthew 12:34). Be bold to stand in your office and protect what God has entrusted to you.

And don't be afraid to make mistakes. Every great leader has made mistakes, and you will too. That doesn't mean you should back down. No, stand up and be bold. God has deemed you fit to be the pastor's wife and stand in that motherhood office; so, don't back down. Rule and rule well—even amid enemies. "The LORD shall send the rod of Your strength out of Zion. Rule in the midst of Your enemies!" (Psalm 110:2 NKJV).

Don't neglect your biological children.

Make sure your biological children are not neglected because of the attention you give your spiritual children. I have noticed that many pastors' wives have powerful spiritual children, but their biological children are uninterested in the things of God. This is because there's prayer at church but not in the home. They are not praying with their children or teaching them how to pray, so there's fire in the ministry but not the home. It is important to have fiery altars in both places to balance the scale.

Don't discuss your marital challenges or home affairs with church members.

Avoid venting your frustrations about your spouse or "running down" the man of God verbally to anyone in the church—regardless of the circumstance. Do not involve church members in your marital or familial challenges—period.

Why? They may take sides even after you have forgiven each other. They may use it against you and your husband. They may gossip and exaggerate what you said resulting in lies spreading throughout the church and on and on.

If the Holy Spirit doesn't reveal it, you never know what a person may do with the information, so be a gatekeeper. Keep the lips (the doors) of your mouth shut to church members when it comes to your marital and familial challenges. Instead, be a spiritual scanner and x-ray machine to help protect your spouse, family, and the ministry. Always ask God to show you people's true motives, even those of the key ministers that serve with you.

Moreover, every pastor's wife must, at all costs, avoid being part of drama in the ministry. Yes, you can expect any institution that involves humans to have drama at some point. However, you, the pastor's wife, should avoid it at all costs.

That takes us back to 1 Timothy 3:2, which says we must be blameless. Strive at all costs to be blameless by avoiding gossip, never sharing your personal problems with church members, and never being involved in he-said-she-said drama.

Don't share what others tell you in confidence.

Because of your position, people will come to you in confidence and share intimate, secret things about their lives. Do your best to keep that confidence. I have learned to avoid sharing what someone tells you with another.

Unfortunately, sometimes you cannot fully avoid sharing some things because they affect the safety or spiritual wellbeing of others, or someone is lying. Sadly, some members never tell the truth. They tell only the side of the story that favors them. I had experienced this repeatedly in ministry until one day my spiritual mother advised me. She gave me wisdom concerning a situation where we had to discipline someone in the church and sit them down from serving.

This person went and told the church a whole different story. There was a lot of gossip and rumors in the church about what happened to her and what was said and done. My spiritual mother was able to stand up and tell me I had made a big mistake and would now have to learn from the situation.

She helped me understand how to better handle such situations. Instead of just sitting a person down from serving in a ministry, call all those working with or under them and hold a meeting to tell them what was done. Then, give the person a leave of absence to fix their character or actions.

Doing this publicly will keep a ministry from falling into the snare of gossip or rumors. When you do it privately, the person can turn around and use it against you, giving everyone a different story. By the time you discover that they have spread wrong information, you will be looking guilty as if you are a criminal, and the person will be looking innocent.

So, as in this example, when certain things happen in ministry, you, as a pastor's wife, are compelled to reveal what you have been keeping private for clarity's sake, to save someone from stumbling, or to avoid confusion. In some instances, it's important to bring to light what has been discussed in private because demonic members know how to use information to their advantage while destroying the pastor, the pastor's wife, or the ministry.

More recently, one of our members started acting very strange, but because I believe in prayer, I prayed about the issue. I believe in motherhood so not all spiritual children are going to be perfect. She told me concerning things in private that were very hurtful and obnoxious. If she had said them to another pastor's wife, they would have walked straight out of the ministry. But I was able to bear with it, believing that God would do a work in her.

To my surprise, this lady mistook my silence for stupidity or my humility for ignorance of what she was trying to do. When she continued to go overboard, I called a meeting and had to tell the people in this meeting some of the exact words she told me in private. By the time I shared what she had said, some people almost fainted and others were on their knees crying. "Pastor, we are sorry you had to listen to all this garbage and go through this," they said. Some even bought me beautiful flowers to comfort me and tell me they loved me. They told me if they were the pastor, that girl would not be in the church anymore.

But I believe in change; I didn't chase her from the ministry but committed her to God in prayer, asking Him to change her. I was compelled to tell the committee members what she had been telling me in my office. This helped to cut down the false information she was spreading.

Such things happen in ministry, but how you handle them matters. Yes, privacy is important, but sometimes when your integrity is on the line, things must come out in "black and white." So, privacy is good but may be difficult in a public institution like church where people manipulate words to suit their situation.

Still, above all, we should uphold privacy when possible. For example, if someone confided in you and left the ministry, you owe them the duty to keep their secrets private. Or if someone is suffering from an affliction or disease that would cause them shame or reproach, you owe them privacy. For example, there are times God has showed me when people are dealing with serious diseases. They're quite a few people I've called into my office to tell them the Lord told me they had one disease or the other, and they left the church out of shame. I was under no obligation or pressure to reveal their secret to anybody just because they left. People's marital and family challenges are another example. A pastor's wife should do her best to uphold confidentiality. She must be able to hold her tongue.

Do use the language of a builder.

You must also be able to use your tongue to build others up, especially those working under your leadership. Don't use inconsiderate language or communicate in a way that demeans other people. The language of a builder is polite, considerate, and flexible. It's cooperative and fosters unity versus disunity. It doesn't make things difficult or complicated.

The language of a builder is "let us," we will," or "we shall," versus "you do it now" or "you have to." The building language is the language of leadership versus the language of a commander. We are leaders and not bosses.

Do have a mentor.

Every pastor's wife needs a mentor who does checks and balances in their life and keeps them accountable. This shows that you are under authority yourself. You cannot compel people to be under authority when you're not; that's not how it works. If you want people to submit to you, then who are you submitting to?

Don't let godly patterns fight you. Every position of authority has a pattern pertaining to it. If you try to break a pattern in a leadership role, the pattern will break you. When it comes to godly leadership, even Jesus Christ submitted to John the Baptist. The Roman centurion was under authority; that is why authority worked in his favor (Matt. 8:9).

So as a pastor's wife, it's very important that you are under authority and submission. Always remember you have many people to hail you but not many to correct you.

When you have a true mentor, they will not be afraid to tell you your errors. The people who tell you about your mistakes and errors are the ones who are making you better, not the people who praise you. The praisers make you confident and sometimes, even arrogant; but the critics are the ones who make you a better person. So, it's a very important thing that every pastor's wife be submitted and accountable, becase in doing so, you are correctable and teachable as you also teach others. Do your best to be mentored and avoid being out of order and out of alignment.

Esther was a queen but still under Mordecai's counsel and mentorship. Even after she became a queen, Mordecai was able to advise her when she was about to make the biggest mistake of her queenship. If she was not submitted to a mentor, she would have missed her mark in the Kingdom (Esther 4:14).

People who miss their mark in life lose their place in life. She was going to die, and her father's house was going to perish. But thanks be to God who gave her a humble spirit so she could listen to authority. So madame pastor's wife, who are you submitted to?

If you don't have an answer to that question, find a mentor at your earliest convenience. I am not trying to rush you because it's a very major decision. Take time to pray as you're looking before you approach someone to be your mentor and covering because it has very serious repercussions. Don't rush to find one because I have made it clear it's a must and one of the sure "dos" of a pastor's wife.

Take careful consideration in prayer before you approach someone for mentorship and spiritual covering. Otherwise, I have seen such things turn very bitter, especially if you did not pray about it and God okayed it. I pray that you'll find a mentor who will: guide you into the path of righteousness, uphold you when you're weak, be bold to tell you the truth, not talk behind you but rather in front of you, not be jealous when God is blessing you, not require you to pay them but rather help you become who God has called you to be, and have joy in seeing you fulfill your destiny. Be blessed as you find one.

Do remain well submitted to your own husband.

However powerful you may be, if you're not submitted to your husband, you're out of order according to the Bible.

> And further, submit to one another out of reverence for Christ. [22] For wives, this means submit to your husbands as to the Lord. [23] For a husband is the head of his wife as

> Christ is the head of the church. He is the Savior of his body, the church. ²⁴ As the church submits to Christ, so you wives should submit to your husbands in everything. ²⁵ For husbands, this means love your wives, just as Christ loved the church. He gave up his life for her ²⁶ to make her holy and clean, washed by the cleansing of God's word. ²⁷ He did this to present her to himself as a glorious church without a spot or wrinkle or any other blemish. Instead, she will be holy and without fault. ²⁸ In the same way, husbands ought to love their wives as they love their own bodies. For a man who loves his wife actually shows love for himself. ²⁹ No one hates his own body but feeds and cares for it, just as Christ cares for the church. ³⁰ And we are members of his body. ³¹ As the Scriptures say, "A man leaves his father and mother and is joined to his wife, and the two are united into one." ³² This is a great mystery, but it is an illustration of the way Christ and the church are one. ³³ So again I say, each man must love his wife as he loves himself, and the wife must respect her husband. (Ephesians 5:21-33 NLT)

Christ's sacrificial love and respectful submission are the wheels that keep a marriage turning in the right direction. They reflect Christ' relationship with His bride, the church and are necessary for you and your husband to remain unified partners as you lead God's people.

In this section, we reviewed the responsibilities of every pastor's wife and provided a list of dos and don'ts in this chapter. Following them will save you unnecessary problems, but there are still unavoidable challenges every pastor's wife will face. We address these battles in the next section.

SECTION THREE: BATTLES EVERY PASTOR'S WIFE FIGHTS

The challenges related to being a lead pastor have been researched and documented. We often hear about thousands of senior pastors leaving the ministry each year, yet we less often hear about the frequency at which pastors' wives want to quit. In the same way that lead pastors face particular challenges and battles, their wives do too.

In this section, we address ten battles every pastor's wife fights at some point and provide solutions for winning the battles, including:

1. Accusations
2. Competition
3. Dishonor
4. Famine
5. Gossip and Hypocrisy
6. Jezebels
7. Loneliness
8. Rebellious Children
9. Strife and Divide and Rule Members
10. Unforgiveness

Chapter 8: Accusations

"When Jesus had raised Himself up and saw no one but the woman, He said to her, "Woman, where are those accusers of yours? Has no one condemned you?"" – *Jesus to the accused woman in Romans 8:10 NKJV*

The enemy has used the weapon of accusations against pastors' wives to silence and diminish them. The Bible says, "Lest Satan should take advantage of us; for we are not ignorant of his devices" (2 Corinthians 2:11 NKJV). Pastors' wives are losing the battle with accusations because they are not updated on the devices and weapons the enemy uses to pull them down, and, in the end, these weapons can keep them from fulfilling their destinies.

The Nature of Accusations

Accusations are allegations made against an individual. They could be false, true, or even partially true. Accusations are one of the most efficient and effective weapons the devil deploys in the lives of many Christians. Through observation during my twenty-three years of salvation and ministry, I have seen how accusations succeed in bringing down many anointed and highly gifted people in the body of Christ, especially pastors' wives.

God does not usually uncover or delight in the weaknesses of His servants. He would rather raise up intercessors to cover their nakedness through prayer than expose them. Therefore, every Christian must understand that accusations don't come from God but from the devil himself because God does not delight in exposing the nakedness of His servants.

Accusation is a great weapon the enemy has used and succeeded in silencing many powerful voices. Accusations instigate the following in Christians' lives:

- They discredit what they do or say. The main agenda of accusations is to damage the integrity of what you say or do.
- They create insecurity and uncertainty. When you are discredited and uncertain, you cannot stand boldly and proclaim the message of the Lord Jesus Christ. You cannot even correct believers if you are uncertain of your credibility. Furthermore, it is impossible to explain yourself to someone who is committed to misunderstanding you or accusing you. When your credibility is under scrutiny, you sometimes keep silent even when God wants to say something through you because everyone, including the chief sinner, has already told you how unworthy you are.
- The weapon of accusation sends many pastors' wives into hiding, and they give up on stirring the gift of God on the inside of them. That is why you find that many pastors' wives take a backseat in the ministry of their husbands; they hate to participate, or they are shy because they have been accused at one point or another. Accusations cause a pastor's wife to feel ashamed whether at fault or not.

I encourage you to overthrow the accuser of the brethren (Revelation 12:10) and stand strong in the liberty of Christ, wherein you were called. Perhaps the accusations are sometimes true, untrue, or possibly even partially true. I want you to understand that everyone makes mistakes. But if you handle your mistakes with humility, your destiny will not be terminated.

Even the biblical fathers of faith made mistakes. God is full of grace, and He gave Abraham another chance (Genesis 12:10-20, Genesis 20:2-7). The accusations against the woman who was caught in adultery were true, but God still gave her another chance (John 8:3-11).

The Bible says, "There is therefore now no condemnation to those who are in Christ Jesus . . ." (Romans 8:1 KJV). When accusations come to condemn people, they achieve their purpose swiftly. Refuse to be silenced and condemned by the accuser. Stand boldly in the liberty that Christ has given you and move on with what God has entrusted to you.

Accusations also come to notify you of how unfit you are for the position you are holding as a pastor's wife. Regardless, you are the best person on planet Earth to stand where you are standing. God has approved of you, and according to heaven, you are the most qualified woman to help the man of God. Whoever is telling you otherwise is not under the influence of the Holy Spirit but the accuser of the brethren, which is a satanic spirit.

> And I heard a loud voice saying in heaven, Now is come salvation, and strength, and the kingdom of our God, and the power of his Christ: for the accuser of our brethren is cast down, which accused them before our God day and

night. (Revelation 12:10 KJV)

Let me reassure you that you are the most suitable helper for that man of God. You are the best candidate for that job or office. Let no one tell you how unqualified or underqualified you are.

The way God selects is different from the way the world makes its choices. This reminds me of a person who once told me, "If I were a pastor's wife like you, I would wear nine-inch heels." I replied, "That is the very reason why you are not, and you will never be a pastor's wife. Because your motive and conception are not Godly." God will not place a person who thinks that way in such a position. It is not for a fashion show but for fulfilling a divine mandate. It is a position to help the called man of God become who God destined him to be.

The accuser is a prosecutor who uses evidence from your past or present mistakes. But by prayer, you can disarm the enemy by nullifying that evidence with the blood of Jesus. Yes, by the blood of Jesus, erase every piece of evidence the devil is using to prosecute you in the spiritual courts. The agenda of the accuser is to discredit you so that people's hearts lose hope and faith in you and instead gain faith and confidence in him. He pokes holes in something solid or legitimate so that you lose credibility, and another can gain momentum instead.

The accuser also focuses on taking followers away from you so that they follow him and not you. Satan instigated the angels in heaven against God; thus, they were cast down from heaven. This war is still ongoing in the present church.

The main reason people still prosecute others for their sins or mistakes is they are looking for a following. To get one, they prey on a pastor's wife's mistakes or weaknesses and magnify them in the eyes of her followers. Usually, if that demonic technique succeeds, the accuser gets a following (just like God lost a third of His angels and Satan gained them) (Revelation 12:9).

If you do not serve God, you will serve the devil—directly or indirectly. If you are not on God's side, you are on the devil's side. This is solidified in Matthew 12:30, which says, "He who is not with Me is against Me, and he who does not gather with Me scatters abroad" (NKJV).

Solutions: Winning the Battle Against Accusations

Petition God. Pray the Word.

I want to encourage every pastor's wife who is facing accusations to stand boldly in the presence of God and petition Him concerning the accuser. When you do, victory is guaranteed, not optional. Pray the Word, invoking Scriptures like Psalm 109 that specifically address accusers.

> Do not keep silent, O God of my praise! ² For the mouth of the wicked and the mouth of the deceitful Have opened against me; They have spoken against me with a lying tongue. ³ They have also surrounded me with words of hatred, And fought against me without a cause. ⁴ In return for my love they are my accusers, But I *give myself to* prayer. ⁵ Thus they have rewarded me evil for good, And hatred for my love. ⁶ Set a wicked man over him, And let an accuser stand at his right hand. ⁷ When he is judged, let him be found guilty, And let his prayer become sin. (Psalm 109:1-7 NKJV)

Also, ask God to silence the mouth of the accuser according to Psalm 31:18, which says, "Let the lying lips be put to silence,

Which speak insolent things proudly and contemptuously against the righteous" (NKJV).

Remember that victory is already promised. You are more than a conqueror.

The Bible calls us more than conquerors. So, for us to thrive, we must conquer accusations. In Revelations 12:10, we see that after the accuser is cast down, God's people go to another level of strength, establishment in ministry, and power.

Turn pain into momentum to press forward.

Another fact to keep in mind is pain is part of the journey. This, however, should not stop us but give us momentum to press on towards the mark of the high calling (Philippians 3:14). Many times, unless the accuser is cast down, we will never experience the full manifestation of salvation, strength, and the Kingdom of God. Revelations 12 says, "The accuser of the brethren has been cast down now, there is salvation, strength and the Kingdom of the Lord our God." So, if you succeed in bringing the accuser down through prayer, you will go to another level.

There are some levels of strength and divine momentum that you only attain once the accuser is cast down. So, when you are faced with accusers, don't look at them as accusers. See them as stepping stones to a higher level.

When you see accusers, see open doors and gates, and press on further in prayer, knowing that when you bring down the accuser, your life will go to another level, and so will your ministry. We have seen this in the lives of many ministers around the world. They were accused, but the minute the accuser was cast down and subdued, their lives never remained the same.

Do not give up in the face of accusations. Take a stand and pray. God's final verdict against accusers is that they will be cast down. You are a conqueror, and you will win!

Chapter 9: Competition

"For we dare not class ourselves or compare ourselves with those who commend themselves. But they, measuring themselves by themselves, and comparing themselves among themselves, are not wise." — Paul in 2 Corinthians 10:12 NKJV

Someone is competing with every pastor's wife even though that pastor's wife is not competing with them. So, knowingly or unknowingly, every pastor's wife ends up in the battlefield called competition, which means someone is walking in rivalry, struggling or battling with them, or striving to outdo them. Sadly, this could sometimes be competition between the pastor and his wife or between church members and the pastor's wife.

No matter how it comes, competition is one of the devil's devices to bring strife. God hates strife and does not operate where that spirit prevails. He wants us all to walk in humility and unity, but strife causes division, which quenches God's spirit in the midst of the congregation. Whatever we do, we must keep away from things like strife, which have their roots in competition.

There are many areas in ministry where you find the brethren competing. Most competition is targeted towards leadership and, more so, the pastor's wife. Members compete for the pastors' attention. They compete with her spiritually to prove they are more anointed; they compete with her wardrobe; they compete with her preaching. Instead of looking up to her as a mother, they compete with her. And if they compete, they are forbidden to tap into the grace on her life. It's more important for congregation members to submit than compete.

Competition carries with it a very dangerous yoke called "I know more; I know better." And this kind of yoke makes people unpastorable, insubordinate, rebellious, and unadvisable. Nobody can tell them what to do.

A lot of pastors' wives battle with competition from ladies in ministry who feel they can preach better, flow better in the anointing, are wiser, taller, or have better physical features. They dress better, wear the best designers, and have better connections. They feel they are more anointed, and their revelations are bigger and greater. Competitive ladies in ministry always thwart the position of a pastor's wife. They downplay her role and give the pastor's wife an attitude—a very nasty attitude.

However, when God was vetting the ministry of the pastor's wife, looks, dress code, level of education, and financial status were not part of His agenda. God looks at the heart and the spiritual substance in someone's life.

The good news for every pastor's wife is there are solutions to deal with such ladies who feel they know more and don't deserve to submit to you, but rather, you deserve to submit to them.

Solutions: Winning the Battle Against Competition

Stand firm, knowing that God saw those other women who compete with you but chose you anyway.

That means something unique about you propelled God to choose you over them. So don't let their competition damage your self-esteem. Do not lower yourself to submit to an "I know more; I know better" lady in the ministry. Pastors' wives and believers alike are not called to submit to style but to spiritual authority and substance that can advance the Kingdom of God.

Do not repay competition with competition.

If you're not careful, it's easy to find yourself competing too. You know you have been drawn into competing when you think things like "what is so and so wearing" while you are getting dressed for church. When you're doing things and considering what they are also doing, you have been seduced into competition. At all costs, do whatever it takes to ensure you don't fall into that trap.

Be confident in who you are and how God has called you. God saw those tall, model-like ladies driving expensive cars with lavish clothes who speak better, have a better accent, and even a better flow of the Spirit. Yet and still, God did not regard them for your office. Therefore, you should not downplay your position for them. Competition is a very unhealthy spirit, and it can cripple the ministry if not cut off in the early stages. As the body of Christ, we are called to completion, not competition.

Think soberly; recognize each body part contributes.

> For I say, through the grace given to me, to everyone who is among you, not to think *of himself* more highly than he ought to think, but to think soberly, as God has dealt to each one a measure of faith. (Romans 12:32 NKJV)

People who compete think more highly of themselves than they ought to and don't understand that every member of the body is important. Yes, someone may speak or dress better or drive a more expensive car, but that does not mean the pastor's wife should be under them. Earthly possessions do not dictate spiritual authority.

No matter how small or insignificant a body part may seem, if it does not function properly, it will affect the entire body. In the same way, every one of us has a special part to play in the ministry. If the hand is competing against the leg, there will not be proper operation. Paul said it this way:

> For as the body is one and has many members, but all the members of that one body, being many, are one body, so also *is* Christ. [13] For by one Spirit we were all baptized into one body—whether Jews or Greeks, whether slaves or free—and have all been made to drink into one Spirit. [14] For in fact the body is not one member but many. [15] If the foot should say, "Because I am not a hand, I am not of the body," is it therefore not of the body? [16] And if the ear should say, "Because I am not an eye, I am not of the body," is it therefore not of the body? [17] If the whole body *were* an eye, where *would be* the hearing? If the whole *were* hearing, where *would be* the smelling? [18] *But now God has set the members, each one of them, in the body just as He pleased.* (1 Corinthians 12:12-18 NKJV, italics added)

Pastor's wife, God set you just as He pleased. You don't have to compete with anyone.

Remember, you are an authority, regardless of what they say or think about you.

Some people may have power and influence due to their accumulated "bling bling." However, wealth doesn't give you spiritual authority. The pastor's wife is an authority.

Stay in your lane.

For proper operation, everyone should respect each other's lane. If I'm in the pastor's wife lane and you're in the praise and worship lane, for God's Spirit to flow mightily among and within us, we need to complete one another rather than compete with one another. We are all workers in the vineyard of God, and He rewards us differently than our way of thinking. He pays those who come at the eleventh hour the same wages as those who came early. He declares, "The last shall be first and the first shall be last." (Matthew 20:16). If you take note of this parable, you will understand that we should not compare ourselves or compete with anyone, but rather focus on our own lane. Jesus said:

> "For the kingdom of heaven is like a landowner who went out early in the morning to hire laborers for his vineyard. ² Now when he had agreed with the laborers for a denarius a day, he sent them into his vineyard. ³ And he went out about the third hour and saw others standing idle in the marketplace, ⁴ and said to them, You also go into the vineyard, and whatever is right I will give you.' So they went. ⁵ Again he went out about the sixth and the ninth hour, and did likewise. ⁶ And about the eleventh hour he went out and found others standing idle, and said to them,'Why have you been standing here idle all day?'⁷ They said to him,'Because no one hired us.'He said to them, 'You also go into the vineyard, and whatever is right you will receive.'⁸ "So when evening had come, the owner of the vineyard said to his steward,'Call the laborers and give them *their* wages, beginning with the last to the first.'⁹ And when those came who *were hired* about the eleventh hour, they each received a denarius. ¹⁰ But when the first came, they supposed that they would receive more; and they likewise received each a denarius. ¹¹ And when they had

received *it*, they complained against the landowner, ¹²saying, 'These last *men* have worked *only* one hour, and you made them equal to us who have borne the burden and the heat of the day.'¹³But he answered one of them and said, 'Friend, I am doing you no wrong. Did you not agree with me for a denarius? ¹⁴Take *what is* yours and go your way. I wish to give to this last man *the same* as to you. ¹⁵Is it not lawful for me to do what I wish with my own things? Or is your eye evil because I am good? ¹⁶So the last will be first, and the first last. For many are called, but few chosen." (Matthew 20:1-16 NKJV)

Whether you work all day or night, or every day and others are not doing so, in the end, we have one reward. In the parable, they all received a denarius, whether they started at age sixteen and someone else started serving at age eighty. We all get the same reward—meaning we all inherit eternal life. There is no need to compete. Instead, we need to stay in our lane and not hinder anyone from working to receive the same reward called eternal life.

Do not allow competition to cut you off from God's presence and blessings.

I beseech every pastor's wife reading this book to avoid competition because when it comes, strife will come, and the anointing of the Holy Spirit will be cut off. The enemy wants to use competition to disconnect you from the anointing, presence, and power of God. As it was with Sarah and Hagar, when competition entered, Hagar was cut off.

Sarah recommended Hagar, but when she was promoted, she began to compete and let her child mock the promised child. Hagar was competing with her mother, and that was a "no-no." Daughters are not to compete with their mothers under any circumstance. Spiritual and biological daughters are not to compete with their mothers—period. As a result, Sarah withdrew her recommendation and demanded that Abraham send Hagar and her son away. She lost the blessing. Competition not only allows strife to enter but also all kinds of sin, including pride, which precedes a great downfall—not just physically but spiritually.

God never created mankind for the purpose of competition but rather to complete, support, and encourage one another. If you are in ministry for the purpose of competition, you are out of alignment and totally misplaced because competition is not from God but the father of lies called the devil.

That is why we must fight to stay out of competition and resist the competitive spirit with all our might. I pray that God gives you the ability to paralyze every competition against you, in Jesus' name.

Stay focused on your assignment; don't let competition waste your time and distract you from weightier, more important matters.

If we do not compete, we'll be able to achieve great things. Competition will distract us from divine purposes and accomplishments. Instead of helping one another, we end up fighting one another, thus hindering us from fulfilling divine purposes and agendas. Competition is very time-wasting.

Before I knew too much about ministry, I used to attend a church and hear these ladies talking about the pastor's wife. They were saying, "Where did she buy that? I want to go and buy it as well." I was offended by this statement because I wouldn't want to wear the same thing my mother wears, unless it happened coincidentally. However, I wouldn't want to wear things to match my spiritual authority. I realized these ladies were always looking for the designers the pastor's wife was wearing so they could buy it and feel equal with her.

I want ladies who have such an attitude and motive to know that clothes don't define people. Positions don't define you. The pastor's wife may be wearing whatever she's wearing, but that's not what defines her.

As I kept observing, I realized that everything the pastor's wife did, these ladies did—but with a wrong motive. They wanted to show her they could also do it but at the end of the day, if we analyzed them and the situation, what did they gain from it? If God was to reward them, what would He render to them for their acts? That is for you to ponder upon.

Remember, competition is a trophyless battle; it is unworthy of your time.

Competition is a trophyless and time-wasting battle; it is senseless and useless. I want you to realize there is no reward after competing (operating in a spirit of competition in ministry). We are better off if we engage in battles that have rewards.

Let's spend our efforts on fruitful battles that have rewards. For example, when David killed Goliath, he became tax-exempt and a son-in-law to the king. He changed his status in society. He became connected in high places. Was that battle worth it? Absolutely, because he gained a lot from slaying Goliath. But what are you gaining after you compete?

One time, a believer tried to convince me that there is healthy and unhealthy competition. I asked what healthy competition means. He said healthy competition motivates you, but I don't believe any Christian should be motivated by competition unless they don't believe in the ministry of the Holy Spirit. These are things that the world says. They are unacceptable in the Kingdom of God, and we should stay away from such thinking at all costs. The Bible commands us to love others as we love ourselves. If you love yourself, you can't compete against yourself. Where there is love, there should be no competition.

Nowadays, the pressure to compete is everywhere. There's competition for who has more social media views, likes, and followers. But remember, when you show up on the day of judgment, the Lord will not be looking at how many followers and Facebook likes you have. Jesus will be looking at your impact and accomplishments according to your predetermined assignment. He'll be looking at how well you fulfilled your destiny and did what you were created to do. So, if competition has distracted your focus, I pray that God will help you to refocus. If you have lost yourself in competition, I pray you fix yourself in Jesus again.

Refuse to allow competition to disqualify you.

When the enemy wants to disqualify a person, he uses the weapon of competition. I pray that you will not be found competing when you should be learning or submitting. If not, you may end up being unstable like Reuben. Genesis 49:4 says, "Unstable as water, you shall not excel, Because you went up to your father's bed; Then you defiled *it*—He went up to my couch" (NKJV). Some people are unstable in ministry because of competition.

To help maintain your focus, revisit the dangers of competition again and again.

The Dangers of Competition

Competition is a:

- Seed of the enemy that gives birth to strife
- Battle that prevents you from tapping into the grace of your spiritual authority
- Source of spiritual defilement, which, if you engage, disqualifies you and moves the hand of God far from you
- Rewardless battle
- Time-wasting battle
- Weapon of disqualification
- Negative force that attracts a curse, not a blessing

In addition to the dangers of competition, always remember to never compete with your elder or spiritual mother or father in the name of grace.

We should learn to keep boundaries and have the grace to accept our level. When you are a son, accept your level as a son. Don't try to be an elder.

Some people you are competing with have a wealth of experience, a track record, and years of mileage in the spirit—both spiritually and ministerially. Some even started praying before you were born, so you must accept that some people have great mileage in the spirit beyond you. They have prayer, fasting, prophetic, and apostolic mileage that you probably don't have yet. Instead of competing, humble yourself and learn from them. It will make you a better person and minister.

Some erroneously think they can use the reasoning that they are of a higher grace than their mothers and fathers to compete with them. I hear people say, "I'm of a higher grace," to cover this up, but we should have a better understanding of grace. It doesn't give us the leverage to compete. God is not the author of confusion. It's a misconception; it's a great error. If you see that, don't be intimidated into not correcting it.

Grace never permits us to compete with our authority, elders, or pastors. Grace came to make us better Christians, not competitive Christians. If the highest grace of all, Jesus, submitted to even a so-called lower grace, John the Baptist, then it is okay to sometimes submit to people who you'll be greater than tomorrow. Of course, Jesus knew He was greater than John the Baptist but still submitted to fulfill all righteousness.

Knowing His stature and greatness, Jesus could have competed with John the Baptist. However, because He was operating in the spirit of holiness, He lowered Himself before a man He knew so well. John the Baptist even tried to stop Him, but He said, "Permit *it to be so* now, for thus it is fitting for us to fulfill all righteousness" (Matthew 3:15 NKJV).

> Then Jesus came from Galilee to John at the Jordan to be baptized by him. [14] And John *tried to* prevent Him, saying, "I need to be baptized by You, and are You coming to me?" [15] But Jesus answered and said to him, "Permit *it to be so* now, for thus it is fitting for us to fulfill all righteousness." Then he allowed Him. (Matthew 3:13-15 NKJV)

A word of caution to male pastors.

Husband-pastor, I hope these Scriptures expose the error of the "I know more; I know better" Christians around your wife and ministry. They come to confuse people by convincing them that they are greater and more anointed, eloquent, prophetic, and apostolic than your wife. Take note of such people.

This is a serious caution to male pastors and men of God. If anyone in your ministry ever stands up to your wife, saying they are better than her, do not fall into this snare and allow them to disrespect her. It is so sad that men of God have fallen into this trap.

According to heaven's books, no one can better help you than your wife. Others may have the money or connections, but your greatest help, according to God's holy plan, is your wife. God saw all those so-called women who probably fuel your car and give you money, but they are not the best help of your ministry, life, and marriage. God chose your wife, so don't fall into the snare of such ladies in the ministry.

I have seen many men fall into this folly. They don't even give their wives opportunities to preach but are busy empowering someone they don't even have a covenant with. It's not wrong, but empower your wife first. As the saying goes, "Charity begins at home." It's not wrong to empower a church member, but it's more important to empower your wife. I've seen many pastors despise their wives and trust church members who afterward leave the ministry in a bad place.

And look out for such characters in the ministry. Don't let them step over or disrespect your wife because once you give them a platform, you have endorsed their mischief and error. Before you know it, the whole ministry will be polluted and defiled by this spirit, which will cripple or destroy it. The day Satan felt he could compete with God was the day he was cast down. He fell like lightning because he wanted to ascend above the stars of the Most High.

So, it clear that daughters should not compete with their mothers, and sons should not compete with their fathers so that the anointing of the Holy Spirit may continue to flow. It is good when there is no competition. Then, we will see honor, and God is drawn to work in a place where there is honor rather than a place of competition.

Chapter 10: Dishonor

"Pay to all what is due: . . ., respect to whom respect, honor to whom honor." Paul in Romans 13:7 AMP

Disrespect can be defined as a lack of courtesy or honor. It occurs when people fail to observe the principle of respect toward an individual.

I have seen many pastors' wives experience disrespect from believers, church members, or even the community at large. It is one of the many adverse issues they battle continually because most believers do not understand why they should honor their pastor's wife. Thus, it is essential that believers and male pastors read this chapter.

Often, people award respect and honor to the man of God but not the woman co-laboring for his success and achievements. I have observed many church members or believers go to extremes in disrespecting pastors' wives by frequently buying presents for the pastor on their birthdays or Christmas but never including his wife. I want everyone reading this book to comprehend that it amounts to disrespect whether you do this intentionally or not. It sends mixed signals to the pastor's wife.

I plead that you respect her by including her in the gift giving whether you think she deserves it or not, because she stands behind your anointed man of God. It is polite and respectful. Your honor and respect for your pastor's wife will earn you more blessings than disrespect ever will.

The irony is that this disrespect comes more frequently from women, which baffles me. Why do women disrespect women and then expect to be met with respect in their life journey or ministry? This is very disturbing. I have witnessed several women who buy a man of God gifts and never take time to also celebrate the woman standing in the gap as his wife. Personally, I define this as unscriptural. It looks spiritual, but it's not biblical.

If you respect Abram, why not respect Sarai? In Genesis 16:2, Sarai advises Abram to lay with her maid, Hagar, so they can have a child by her. It was Sarai's recommendation that earned Hagar a place in Abram's life. Other than that, it is not written or recorded anywhere in Scripture that Abram admired or considered Hagar in any way—she was considered only because Sarai, his wife, suggested her.

But in Genesis 16:4, the Bible says that after Hagar conceived, she despised Sarai. She did not recognize that it was Sarai's advice and surrendering her own husband to her that brought her to the position of conception in the first place. This reminds me of many believers who despise a pastor's wife or even hate recognizing her after getting a miracle or breakthrough. Yet, in many cases, they get or earn a miracle because of the intercessions or petitions of a pastor's wife. It was Sarai's petition to her husband that earned Hagar a pregnancy. But as soon as she conceived, she began to disrespect, dishonor, and despise the source of her blessing.

Hagar's actions reaped repercussions. Believers ought to

understand that there can be serious repercussions when you hold a pastor's wife in contempt. Consider the passage in Genesis 16, as it highlights some of the consequences of dishonoring a pastor's wife.

> Now Sarai, Abram's wife, had borne him no children. And she had an Egyptian maidservant whose name was Hagar. ² So Sarai said to Abram, "See now, the Lord has restrained me from bearing children. Please, go in to my maid; perhaps I shall obtain children by her." And Abram heeded the voice of Sarai. ³ Then Sarai, Abram's wife, took Hagar her maid, the Egyptian, and gave her to her husband Abram to be his wife, after Abram had dwelt ten years in the land of Canaan. ⁴ So he went in to Hagar, and she conceived. And when she saw that she had conceived, her mistress became despised in her eyes. ⁵ Then Sarai said to Abram, "My wrong be upon you! I gave my maid into your embrace; and when she saw that she had conceived, I became despised in her eyes. The Lord judge between you and me." ⁶ So Abram said to Sarai, "Indeed your maid is in your hand; do to her as you please." And when Sarai dealt harshly with her, she fled from her presence. ⁷ Now the Angel of the Lord found her by a spring of water in the wilderness, by the spring on the way to Shur. ⁸ And He said, "Hagar, Sarai's maid, where have you come from, and where are you going?" She said, "I am fleeing from the presence of my mistress Sarai." ⁹ The Angel of the Lord said to her, "Return to your mistress, and submit yourself under her hand." (Genesis 16:1-9 NKJV)

Make sure you weigh the consequences of dishonoring your pastor's wife.

Consequences of dishonoring a pastor's wife:

1. You can lose favor. In Genesis 16:5, Hagar lost favor before her mistress, Sarai.

2. You expose yourself to harsh spiritual conditions or climates. In Genesis 16:6, the Bible says Sarai dealt harshly with Hagar and she fled to the wilderness which is a harsh climatical situation because there is dryness; she could no longer enjoy the supply of her mistress' house. Hagar, who once had abundance under a blessed woman's house or covering, was now in the wilderness scrambling for water. She was struggling to get the things she once received with ease when she honored and respected Sarai.

3. You lose proximity, position, and protection. Hagar lost proximity to her mistress. Once, she had been close to Sarai, serving her, but she was cast out after her disrespect. She lost her placement or position because of her disrespect and dishonor. She could no longer serve as a maid unless she humbled herself and submitted to her mistress—not Abraham. Likewise, when you don't submit to your pastor's wife but rather despise and disrespect her, you lose your place of protection and open yourself up to attacks. You lose your covering because there are things God is protecting you from because of her continual intercession and petitions to God. Disrespect causes many believers to face financial, spiritual, and marital dryness or a wilderness, which is where Hagar found herself. Let me reiterate to every reader that disrespect will attract dryness

in your ministry, marriage, and other areas of your life.

4. You move God to come down and humble or humiliate you to unexpected lengths. In Genesis 16:9, the angel of the Lord commands Hagar to return to Sarai, who she was running from, so as to once again submit herself to her. In other words, God humbled Hagar before the very woman she was despising, disrespecting, and dishonoring. In some circumstances, people leave God with no option but to humble them with His superior and supernatural power like he did in Hagar's case. This reminds me of a story my spiritual mother, Dr. Adesuwa Onaiwu of blessed memory, once told me before she went to be with the Lord. A lady once walked into the church while she was preaching and greatly despised her and regretted coming to church that evening. A few weeks down the road, she was struck with a lot of boil-like swellings on her body. They kept worsening until she started going to the very woman she despised on the pulpit for prayer. After a few prayer encounters with the woman she despised, the lady was miraculously healed. She asked herself, why did I despise her? This is a question for all women to ponder. Why do women despise women? The point of the story is that disrespect will cause God's mighty hand to come down and humble you. Remember, God resists the proud but gives grace to the humble (James 4:6).

5. You can open the door to premature death. In 2 Kings 2:23, youth came out and despised and disrespected the man of God, Elisha, calling him names, jeering, and making fun of

his bald head. The Bible says a bear came out and mauled the youth. They lost their lives due to their disrespect. These youth would not have died prematurely had they honored the man of God. In Acts 5:3, where Ananias and Sapphira, his wife, lied to the Holy Spirit, we also see that disrespect can further premature death. When you lie, it's a sign of disrespect and causes death. People who honor the Holy Spirit don't lie. They respect Him enough to always speak the truth.

6. You can contract spiritual leprosy. Dishonor opens you up to evil spiritual illnesses like leprosy, which causes de-sensitivity to the Spirit of God. Leprosy is a disease that numbs your nerves so that you lose feeling. Therefore, spiritual leprosy de-sensitizes your spirit man so that you can no longer feel or sense the move of the Holy Spirit. You no longer have sensitivity to the voice of God. Once you lose sensitivity to God, sin becomes the norm because de-sensitization to the Holy Spirit causes a lack of sensitivity to sin and wrongdoing. The minute one loses the fear of God or the sensitivity of sin and wrong, the fear of God is out of the window.

Before you engage in acts and behaviors of disrespect, weigh the consequences adequately. Disrespect can cost you the throne like it cost Vashti the throne. It can cost you doors, gates, relationships, and destinies.

Unexpected consequences of dishonor.

It's a paradox, but disrespect, though universally unwanted, can sometimes work to the advantage of the person being disrespected. Throughout Scripture, we see disrespect triggering God's intervention, His power manifesting, and wickedness being overturned on the victim's behalf.

There are several circumstances in the Bible where disrespect was a catalyst for big changes. If Haman had never disrespected Mordecai or the Jews, Haman would have retained his position. Mordecai never would've risen to prominence in the Persian kingdom. Disrespect was a major factor that helped Mordecai attain heights and levels of power and authority in the kingdom. If Vashti had not disrespected the king, there would have been no opening for Esther to rise to the throne. If Pharaoh had not disrespected the commands of God through Moses, we would never have beheld the outstretched arm of God, especially His wonder-working power in making a highway in the Red Sea. If Peninnah had not disrespected Hannah due to her barrenness, Samuel, the great prophetic voice, would not have come. In this case, God used Peninnah's disrespect as a birth pain to provoke Hannah to cry before God to bring forth a son.

Understanding the Source of Dishonor

Every believer must grasp the severity of disrespecting another believer, especially one in authority. It is a very poisonous ingredient that can wreak havoc in their lives. I have done a few background checks on why Christians carry around this poison called dishonor, and I discovered that some people disrespect others due to their poor background or upbringing. They are brought up in poverty, so the minute they gain some money, they tend to look down on others because all they see is their great achievements and accomplishments. They despise, disrespect, and dishonor others.

Another discovery I made as to why people live in dishonor is that success manipulates them and stirs up disrespect in them. I cannot forget a personal story of a lady I once prayed for and prophesied to about a financial wind that was coming her way if she obeyed God in a certain area of her life. When she took the step I told her to take, there was such a big, sudden financial influx. At first, she was grateful and sent seeds in appreciation. But as time went on, because of her financial contribution to my ministry, her ego was elevated to heights unimaginable to the extent that she talked to me in a very disrespectful and dishonorable way. I want to believe that the success she acquired financially in that short span of time had now entered her heart and mind.

She grew wings, and her heart was lifted up within her. Her conceitedness grew to an extent where she no longer cared how she addressed the same woman of God who God used to release that financial blessing she was enjoying. This lady once said, "Pastor Bella, you taught me how to pray, but I am now way better than you." Wow! What a statement. In fact, her theology is not even right. Why? Because the Bible clearly states in Luke 6:40, "No student is better than their teacher, and no servant is better than their master."

When I removed this lady's proximity to me because of her disrespect, within a few weeks, she was back to the financial distress she was in before. This is a lesson to every believer. Learn to always respect and honor people that God uses to propel you forward into destiny. Disrespect can cause you to lose the blessing of God that He bestows on you.

I have heard people argue that God gave them the blessing, not the servant of God. Yes, that is undeniable, but He used human vessels to convey the blessings—not even angelic vessels, though He could. So, aren't we supposed to honor and respect God's chosen vessels after they perform their God-given assignments? My answer is yes. We must honor and respect them because even God Himself honors them by choosing to work through them. If God honors them, why not you and me, the recipients of the miracles?

God uses people to bless people, so honor whoever He has used in your life. Don't dare to disrespect them. Otherwise, you might lose it all. When Ruth honored Naomi, she gained it all. Yet because Orpah left, she lost it all because we do not even hear about her after her departure (Ruth 1:6-14). Sometimes, your Naomi (pastor's wife) could be going through difficulty, but don't turn your back on her then because you cannot see anything good in her anymore. Just like Ruth, have faith—see beyond the difficulty and cling to your destiny helpers until they propel you to the levels God has assigned them to propel you.

Be determined to walk in honor.

Chapter 11: Famine

"Who shall separate us from the love of Christ? Shall tribulation, or distress, or persecution, or famine, or nakedness, or peril, or sword?" — Paul in Romans 8:35 NKJV

Although it's not popular to admit, every pastor, pastor's wife, minister, and believer will face famine at some point in life. Famine is a drought, shortage, scarcity, or need for something that cannot be supplied. Indeed, everyone experiences famine at some point in life. If you are one of the rare people who have never experienced it, expect to at some point in life or ministry. That is not a negative prophecy. Servant of God, don't think this strange.

The Bible even says there will be famine in the last days. Paul says that even famine cannot separate us from the love of God (Romans 8:35), and he speaks about often being in affliction and hunger. He says:

> Are they servants of Christ? I know I sound like a madman, but I have served him far more! I have worked harder, been put in prison more often, been whipped times without number, and faced death again and again. [24] Five different times the Jewish leaders gave me thirty-nine

lashes. ²⁵ Three times I was beaten with rods. Once I was stoned. Three times I was shipwrecked. Once I spent a whole night and a day adrift at sea. ²⁶ I have traveled on many long journeys. I have faced danger from rivers and from robbers. I have faced danger from my own people, the Jews, as well as from the Gentiles. I have faced danger in the cities, in the deserts, and on the seas. And I have faced danger from men who claim to be believers but are not. ²⁷ I have worked hard and long, enduring many sleepless nights. I have been hungry and thirsty and have often gone without food. I have shivered in the cold, without enough clothing to keep me warm. ²⁸ Then, besides all this, I have the daily burden of my concern for all the churches. (2 Corinthians 11:23-28 NLT)

Paul has seen abundance and lack; he knows how to be abased and abound (Philippians 4:12). He suffered various kinds of famine. Sometimes, there was a lack of food. Other times, there was a lack of help. There are physical and spiritual famines.

Pastor's wives experience varied famines. Many experience the spiritual famine of lack of helpers. They hardly find trustworthy people with genuine hearts to help them carry the burden of ministry. They may also experience financial famine, especially if their family depends on the ministry for income. There is also the famine of having no one to stand with you in times of crisis or persecution for the work's sake. Paul also experienced this and said, "The first time I was brought before the judge, no one came with me. Everyone abandoned me. May it not be counted against them" (2 Timothy 4:16 NLT).

The agendas and reasons why God allows famines are as varied as the types of famine the pastor's wife may endure. Through research, I discovered that a famine can either be orchestrated by God or the devil to achieve certain results in a nation, individual, marriage, home, church, or ministry. So before you respond negatively to a famine, consider the greater agenda for its arrival.

Reasons for Famines

The enemy can use famine to tempt you to return to bondage and miss your blessing.

Sometimes, financial famines cause God's servants to leave the ministry and return to the marketplace. Other times, a lack of helpers can lead to returning to the world for solace. In Genesis 26, Isaac endured a famine and was confronted with a choice to return to Egypt.

> There was a famine in the land, besides the first famine that was in the days of Abraham. And Isaac went to Abimelech king of the Philistines, in Gerar. ²Then the LORD appeared to him and said: "Do not go down to Egypt; live in the land of which I shall tell you. ³Dwell in this land, and I will be with you and bless you; for to you and your descendants I give all these lands, and I will perform the oath which I swore to Abraham your father. ⁴And I will make your descendants multiply as the stars of heaven; I will give to your descendants all these lands; and in your seed all the nations of the earth shall be blessed; ⁵because Abraham obeyed My voice and kept My charge, My commandments, My statutes, and My laws." ⁶So Isaac dwelt in Gerar. (Genesis 26:1-6 NKJV)

Isaac could have given in to the financial pressure the famine caused and fled to Egypt. However, God told him to dwell where the famine was, and He would bless him in that same land. Sometimes, the devil uses demonic famine and hard situations to get you out of position for a pending blessing. If God is not saying you should move, don't give in to the pressure. Because Isaac stayed and sowed in the land of famine, God richly blessed him. "Then Isaac sowed in that land, and reaped in the same year a hundredfold; and the LORD blessed him. The man began to prosper, and continued prospering until he became very prosperous" (Genesis 26:12-13 NKJV).

Don't let seasons of famine get you out of position for your pending blessing. Stand in the famine, believe God, sow seeds, and you will be blessed.

God may use famine to get you to acknowledge His sovereignty and depend more deeply on Him.

Ahab was a wicked king of Israel. He ". . . did what was evil in the LORD's sight, even more than any of the kings before him. And as though it were not enough to follow the sinful example of Jeroboam, he married Jezebel, the daughter of King Ethbaal of the Sidonians, and he began to bow down in worship of Baal" (1 Kings 16 30-31 NLT). He worshipped Baal and set up an evil altar for Baal in Israel.

As a result, Elijah prophesied a famine on the land saying to Ahab, "*As* the LORD God of Israel lives, before whom I stand, there shall not be dew nor rain these years, except at my word" (1 Kings 17:1 NKJV). Elijah knew Ahab and the people who followed him would not acknowledge God's sovereignty without a mighty display of power. So, he called for a famine.

Water was scarce, to the extent that brooks dried up. There wasn't enough water to feed Israel's livestock because there had been no rain for years (1 Kings 17:7, 18:5). However, Eliah challenged the prophets of Baal by saturating the altars with water and declaring that the God who answered by fire on the altar was the true and living God.

The prophets of Baal cried out to their demon god to no avail. Jehovah, the true and living God answered Elijah by fire, and Elijah executed all the prophets of Baal. It was then, and only then that the people acknowledged God.

> Now when all the people saw *it*, they fell on their faces; and they said, "The LORD, He *is* God! The LORD, He *is* God! ⁴⁰ And Elijah said to them, "Seize the prophets of Baal! Do not let one of them escape!" So they seized them; and Elijah brought them down to the Brook Kishon and executed them there. ⁴¹ Then Elijah said to Ahab, "Go up, eat and drink; for *there is* the sound of abundance of rain." (1 Kings 18:39-41 NKJV)

The famine ended after the people acknowledged that the Lord is God. Elijah publicly executed judgment on the prophets of Baal. Rain was released, and the people's hearts turned back to God. The famine was a tool to prove God's supremacy and sovereignty to everyone.

Even though we encounter famine, God does not forget us. Like the ravens that fed Elijah, God knows how to release divine supply and show us again and again that He is the sovereign, almighty, all-powerful God. In times of famine, fix your faith in the God who answers by fire.

The enemy can use famine as retaliation.

Elisha's greatness as a prophet was demonstrated by his ability to see in the Spirit and how God backed his prayers. He once delivered the Arameans into Israel's hands by praying that God would strike them blind. God answered him and because they could not see, he led them to Samaria instead of Israel. As a result, the king of Israel captured the Aramean troops and sent them back to their country.

> As the Aramean army advanced toward him, Elisha prayed, "O LORD, please make them blind." So the LORD struck them with blindness as Elisha had asked. [19] Then Elisha went out and told them, "You have come the wrong way! This isn't the right city! Follow me, and I will take you to the man you are looking for." And he led them to the city of Samaria. [20] As soon as they had entered Samaria, Elisha prayed, "O LORD, now open their eyes and let them see." So the LORD opened their eyes, and they discovered that they were in the middle of Samaria. [21] When the king of Israel saw them, he shouted to Elisha, "My father, should I kill them? Should I kill them?" [22] "Of course not!" Elisha replied. "Do we kill prisoners of war? Give them food and drink and send them home again to their master." [23] So the king made a great feast for them and then sent them home to their master. After that, the Aramean raiders stayed away from the land of Israel. (2 Kings 6:18-23 NLT)

Elisha's ministry brought salvation and deliverance to the nation. The Arameans stayed away, but it was only for a time. "Some time later, however, King Ben-hadad of Aram mustered his entire army and besieged Samaria. As a result, there was a great famine in the city. The siege lasted so long that a donkey's head sold for eighty pieces of silver, and a cup of dove's dung sold for five pieces of silver" (2 Kings 6:24-25 NLT).

The King of Aram brought the famine to punish Israel for the embarrassment Elisha's prophetic insight inflicted on them. It was a retaliation planned for an opportune time. Aram's siege lasted so long that food became extremely unaffordable and so scarce that people were selling dove's dung to eat.

Still, that's not all. The famine was so severe that women were eating their children. When the king heard this, he vowed to have

Elisha killed.

> But then the king asked, "What is the matter?" She replied, "This woman said to me: 'Come on, let's eat your son today, then we will eat my son tomorrow.' ²⁹ So we cooked my son and ate him. Then the next day I said to her, 'Kill your son so we can eat him,' but she has hidden her son." ³⁰ When the king heard this, he tore his clothes in despair. And as the king walked along the wall, the people could see that he was wearing burlap under his robe next to his skin. ³¹ "May God strike me and even kill me if I don't separate Elisha's head from his shoulders this very day," the king vowed. (2 Kings 6:28-30 NLT)

Notice that even though Elisha's prophetic gift once saved the nation, the king now wants to kill him. You may endure famine at no fault of your own. It's only that the enemy retaliates against your ministry and uses others who misunderstand and misrepresent you.

God intervened in Elisha's situation, turning it around, and He can do the same for you. And just as Elisha prophesied the famine, he also prophesied its end, saying:

> "Elisha replied, "Listen to this message from the LORD! This is what the LORD says: By this time tomorrow in the markets of Samaria, six quarts of choice flour will cost only one piece of silver, and twelve quarts of barley grain will cost only one piece of silver."² The officer assisting the king said to the man of God, "That couldn't happen even if the LORD opened the windows of heaven!" But Elisha replied, "You will see it happen with your own eyes, but you won't be able to eat any of it!" (2 Kings 7:1-2 NLT)

Keep using your gift. Keep walking in your grace. Even if some retaliate, God will defend you if you remain faithful to Him.

Chapter 12: Gossip and Hypocrisy

"A devious person spreads quarrels. A gossip separates the closest of friends." – Solomon in Proverbs 16:29, GW God's Word Translation

Every pastor's wife I know has been the topic of church gossip. The same church members who smile and greet you often speak about you behind your back. They are pretenders and actors full of hypocrisy. This is a common battle, and pastors' wives often ignore it. However, there are times when hypocrisy and gossip must be confronted to avoid violations of protocol and protect the church. I will give you an example.

I introduced a wonderful pastor friend of mine to my late spiritual mother, Dr. Adesuwa Onaiwu. After a short while, that pastor friend was not communicating with me much, which was okay because I thought she was busy. She even started coming to the United States and did not call as soon as she landed as she had done in the past. Initially, that didn't bother me either.

My spiritual mother called me on various occasions to ask if I had heard from my pastor friend, but I didn't know why. Later, she disclosed that my so-called pastor friend had been calling her all the time, wanting to talk with her. However, she wanted to know if she was in touch with me. I said she wasn't, and that was always a surprise to my spiritual mother. She later told me she was very upset once she realized my pastor friend wasn't communicating with me.

My spiritual mother wanted to confront her about her hypocrisy. Why? The real reason she pursued my spiritual mother was that she wanted her to give her opportunities to minister. This is how I realized she was not genuine. Although her words were always as smooth as butter, she was exposed.

You must follow the proper protocols in ministry. Jesus said you're a thief and a robber if you don't go through the proper door. She stopped talking to me, perhaps because she didn't want me to know she wanted opportunities to ministry or thought her chances would be blocked if I was involved. My spiritual mother told her she could not go behind my back; that is how she lost ground.

Some people go to the extent of gossiping about you to whoever they're trying to get opportunities from. That's why many ministers are afraid of introducing people to their contacts. A good friend in Europe recently invited an African pastor to minister. By the end of the conference, he had befriended everyone, taken their contacts, and was gossiping about the people who had invited him and paid for his ticket to come. This is highly demonic.

When someone opens a door or trusts you with their pulpit, don't become greedy or unfaithful and try to gain control using gossip or hypocrisy. Remember, the people you're gossiping about are the same ones God used to introduce you to the people you're conniving with. You don't destroy relationships that give you opportunities; you build and protect them. However, modern-day greed and foolishness have taught many ministers the demonic way of gaining ground and territory.

If God called you, He has a particular harvest field for you. Don't fish in another man's waters or harvest in another man's field. Look for the harvest wherever God will show you, but don't go to another man's field and begin to take your harvest. Remember, what you sow, you will reap. If you do it in someone else's field, someone will come do it to you, pressed down, shaken together, and running over. So be careful what you do when you're invited.

> When you are invited to eat with a king, use your best manners. ² Don't go and stuff yourself! That would be just the same as cutting your throat. ³ Don't be greedy for all of that fancy food! It may not be so tasty. ⁴ Give up trying so hard to get rich. ⁵ Your money flies away before you know it, just like an eagle suddenly taking off. (Proverbs 23:1-5 CEV)

When you're invited to minister, use your best manners—not just at the dining table but on the pulpit. Recently, I heard of a man of God who was invited and told everything was at his service during his time of ministry. So, he also used the sisters who were serving in that conference as amenities. That was how his ministry ended. Don't say one thing and live your life another way; be the first follower of the Jesus you preach.

Unfortunately, some ministers have opened the door to the spirit of hypocrisy and gossip by giving self-seeking people the platform to operate or engaging in gossip themselves. The best way to win this battle against gossip and hypocrisy is to refuse to open the door and entertain it. Once you don't dance to its music, it fades quickly without gaining attention or relevance.

My spiritual mother refused to open the door, entertain nonsense, and dance to its music, and the name of the Lord she carried was not negated. Our relationship stayed intact and pure until the last day of her departure. So, as a pastor's wife, do not allow gossip and hypocrisy to come between you and your god-ordained relationships. Do whatever it takes to preserve, protect, and undergird relationships, and hypocrisy will not have the ability to destroy them.

Here's another important thing to note about hypocrisy. When people are deceptive and hypocritical, their hearts don't match their words.

Excessive praise sometimes masks hypocrisy.

Pastors' wives should be very careful with the people who praise them excessively. Sometimes, they don't mean it. So don't be carried away with praise. The Bible says some people's words are as smooth as butter, but their hearts are full of war.

> *The words* of his mouth were smoother than butter, But war *was* in his heart; His words were softer than oil, Yet they *were* drawn swords. (Psalms 55:21 NKJV)

> His talk is smooth as butter, yet war is in his heart; his words are more soothing than oil, yet they are drawn swords. (Psalms 55:21 NIV)

You can't trust anyone who always praises you but never tells you that you do some things wrong. They may use the praises to destroy you or blind you to their true character. This means they speak like friends, but in their hearts, you are their enemy. They wear masks or veils to conceal their true feelings and attitudes toward you. This is hypocrisy, and Jesus described it this way: "Hypocrites! For you are so careful to clean the outside of the cup and the dish, but inside you are filthy—full of greed and self-indulgence!" (Matthew 23:25 NLT).

Today, as in the days of Jesus Christ, the people society deems as

God-fearing are not. They are far from being holy and God-fearing. That means we may think some people in ministry are close to God, but they are closer to the devil. That is why John the Baptist said, "You brood of vipers!" (Matthew 3:7). That tells you that hypocrisy is highly present in the ministry, so as a pastor's wife, please don't use your natural eyes to observe the true identity of people.

God had to open Ezekiel's eyes to see the true nature of some of Israel's people and elders. They were supposed to facilitate and invite the glory of God into His temple. Instead, they were engaged in abominable acts and idolatry.

> And behold, the glory of the God of Israel *was* there, like the vision that I saw in the plain. ⁵ Then He said to me, "Son of man, lift your eyes now toward the north." So I lifted my eyes toward the north, and there, north of the altar gate, was this image of jealousy in the entrance. ⁶ Furthermore He said to me, "Son of man, do you see what they are doing, the great abominations that the house of Israel commits here, to make Me go far away from My sanctuary? Now turn again, you will see greater abominations." ⁷ So He brought me to the door of the court; and when I looked, there was a hole in the wall. ⁸ Then He said to me, "Son of man, dig into the wall"; and when I dug into the wall, there was a door. ⁹ And He said to me, "Go in, and see the wicked abominations which they are doing there." ¹⁰ So I went in and saw, and there — every sort of creeping thing, abominable beasts, and all the idols of the house of Israel, portrayed all around on the walls. ¹¹ And there stood before them seventy men of the elders of the house of Israel, and in their midst stood Jaazaniah the son of Shaphan. Each man had a censer in his hand, and a thick cloud of incense went up. ¹² Then He said to me, "Son of man, have you seen what the elders of

> the house of Israel do in the dark, every man in the room of his idols? For they say, 'The LORD does not see us, the LORD has forsaken the land.' " [13] And He said to me, "Turn again, *and* you will see greater abominations that they are doing." [14] So He brought me to the door of the north gate of the LORD's house; and to my dismay, women were sitting there weeping for Tammuz. [15] Then He said to me, "Have you seen *this*, O son of man? Turn again, you will see greater abominations than these." [16] So He brought me into the inner court of the LORD's house; and there, at the door of the temple of the LORD, between the porch and the altar, *were* about twenty-five men with their backs toward the temple of the LORD and their faces toward the east, and they were worshiping the sun toward the east. [17] And He said to me, "Have you seen *this*, O son of man? Is it a trivial thing to the house of Judah to commit the abominations which they commit here? For they have filled the land with violence; then they have returned to provoke Me to anger. Indeed they put the branch to their nose. [18] Therefore I also will act in fury. My eye will not spare nor will I have pity; and though they cry in My ears with a loud voice, I will not hear them." (Ezekiel 8:4-18 NKJV)

The people who should have been bringing down glory and revival were the very people blocking and hindering revival with their secret, obnoxious lives. These elders seemed to be the most god-fearing people in public, but they were not God-worshippers at all. They were idolaters. They were not for God; they were for the devil. They were the evil ones, so we see the hypocrisy of the elders of Israel.

If a man is unafraid to betray our great, big God, what about men? Likewise, if someone, for example, a church member, is not afraid to betray their pastor, they will not be afraid to do it to anyone else. If they are willing to betray their spiritual father or mother, what makes you think they won't betray someone else? That is what I call cheap mathematics in ministerial ethics.

Every pastor's wife must be mindful of such hypocritical people because they are in every ministry and church. May God give you the spirit of discernment to be able to see them and carefully navigate your way around. Sometimes you can't get rid of such people because they are part of your journey and training. God will take away some enemies but leave some. Even though you pray that God removes them, He will not because some people are His weapon of training for you.

Solutions for Overcoming Hypocrisy

Be prayerful and read the word of God often.

Don't allow yourself to be distracted. The mission of gossip and hypocrisy is to cause confusion in the house of God among the brethren, ministers, and members. Refuse to be distracted, in Jesus' name. Refuse to be confused in the house of God. Know who you worship and stand for Him. Once you show strength and focus, the mission of hypocrisy will be aborted.

Don't believe everything you hear. People lie to pastors and leaders, too.

I don't believe everything I hear. I may listen, but I don't believe it until I prove it myself. Even if you tell me, I may behave as if I know nothing when talking to the involved parties. If most people knew what I have heard about them, they would shy away. But unless I prove it, I protect that knowledge very highly.

Many times, you cannot avoid people bringing you gossip because of the position you hold as a church leader, but it's your responsibility to not act on it or even transmit it. Also, do not allow it to be a basis of your decisions and direction in ministry.

Some people come to tell you a point of concern or something to be careful of because you are the pastor's wife. However, always take the battle back to God and ask, "God, is this from you or the enemy? Is this true or untrue?" Lean on the Holy Spirit for direction. God is still speaking today; He is still revealing the truth. The Holy Spirit is the Spirit of Truth, so always trust Him to guide you in all truth—always. If you do, you will win the battle of hypocrisy.

The Battle of Gossip

Now, let's address the battle of gossip, which is related to hypocrisy. Gossip and hypocrisy are highly connected because gossip gives birth to hypocrisy and vice versa. Hypocrisy brings about gossip. When you are true and sincere, there is nothing to gossip about. And if you also don't gossip, there's nothing to be hypocritical about.

Gossip is when:

- Utterances that may be true or untrue are said behind someone's back and have a tendency to spread quickly.
- People say good things to your face, but in your absence, or behind your back, they say horrible things.
- There is willful engagement in the use of words to harm another, which is evil.
- People spread idle talk or rumors, especially about the personal or private affairs of others.[2]
- There are whispers, rumors, tales, discussions, or

---

[2] Dictionary.com, s.v., "gossip," accessed August 2, 2024, https://www.dictionary.com/browse/gossip.

scandals.

Because church is a human institution, one of its biggest weaknesses is he-said-she-said drama. It exists in all churches. Whether you like it or not, there is somebody who will say something about you behind your back in every church.

Gossip is demonically orchestrated. It is a force and a demon that many churches need to learn to fight. Personally, I have traveled quite a bit, and this demon seems to be in every church or ministry. Some ministries have been good at taming it, but someone will always say something behind your back—it may be good or bad. Regardless, it's still gossip.

Another mission of gossip is to make you err, but again, if you don't depend on it as your standard to do things, make decisions, or take directions, it will not have you in its prison. You will not be one of its victims.

Yes, you will have to face this battle at some point because people gossip about pastor's wives, their spouses, children, and families all the time. Still, you can win this battle and emerge with victory.

Many critics gossip, which is one way they gain ground in the ministry. They manipulate through gossip because that he-said-she-said whispering is always done in secret—in the shadows. They must keep their gossip a secret for it to continue to gain ground against its culprit because, most times, it's not true or accurate anyway. I have a story to tell that resonates with this truth.

A while ago, before my husband and I began in ministry, he was under the leadership of a certain man of God and had a certain circle of friends. A few days before something happened, the Holy Spirit whispered to me about one particular friend. He said,

"Warn your husband that that man is not his friend." I went back to the Holy Spirit and asked, "Why do you say he's not his friend? They are always hanging out together."

The Holy Spirit showed me this man was jealous of my husband. At that time, we had nothing, so I wondered what specifically he could be jealous of. The Holy Spirit said he was jealous of my husband's car, which wasn't the type that could draw attention at all. He also said he was jealous of my husband because he had a beautiful wife, and he didn't.

A few days later, my husband couldn't pick me up from work because he was delayed somewhere and asked this friend to pick me up. As we were driving in the car, he started crossing boundaries with me, trying to touch me where he should not. I was so angry and told him to stop the car so I could get out. However, he simply apologized and played things cool.

Nonetheless, he kept calling and telling me not to tell my husband. The Holy Spirit used this to expose him and confirm the few things He had shown me about him days before. When he realized I was not the kind he could sleep with, he devised another strategy to take down my husband.

He told his pastor rumors concerning my husband. Unfortunately, that senior pastor believed the gossip and acted upon it to aggressively attack my husband. My husband did not fight back; he simply stayed away.

A few weeks later, the senior pastor learned that my husband's so-called friend had his own issues, and he had been misled so terribly. He had hurt an innocent person. He started calling me and asking me to plead with my husband to forgive him and come back. He admitted to me that he was wrong. He didn't know the competition that was going on and the issues this gentleman was having with my husband.

Unfortunately, it was too bad and too late. This pastor had already acted on gossip and false accusations, and sometimes, it is almost impossible to reverse the effects of certain things done after a gossip attack. Please know that gossip can close doors that apologies cannot reopen. So, that pastor lost a wonderful treasure so quickly over something instigated by gossip. He regretted it dearly but could not gain it back. Avoid making decisions based on gossip.

As with dishonor, human beings should avoid gossip at all costs. However, God is the exception to that rule. He used gossip as a weapon of spiritual warfare to destroy an arrogant and confident enemy. Sennacherib was a boastful king and confident enemy against God's children, but God used a rumor, another word for gossip, to destroy his plan against the children of God. (2 Kings 19:7, Isaiah 37: 7).

> And Isaiah said to them, "Thus you shall say to your master, 'Thus says the LORD: "Do not be afraid of the words which you have heard, with which the servants of the king of Assyria have blasphemed Me. ⁷Surely I will send a spirit upon him, and he shall hear a rumor and return to his own land; and I will cause him to fall by the sword in his own land." ' " (2 Kings 19:6-7 NKJV)

In this passage of Scripture, you can see that, like dishonor, God sometimes uses rumors to achieve divine purpose and progress and to defeat His enemies. He can take what the enemy meant for evil and turn it for good.

Solutions: How to handle the unending problem of gossip in ministry.

Audit your inner circle.

Every pastor's wife is encouraged to have an inner circle within an inner circle. This means you may have many friends but trust only a few and be genuinely open to fewer who are truly sisters. Open the intimate parts of your life only to those you know well and have scanned very well in the spirit because every inner circle can be infiltrated by a Judas Iscariot.

Jesus had an inner circle within his inner circle, which means He had twelve disciples, but He had an inner circle of three that He took to the mountain of transfiguration. That was the inner circle within His inner circle. You can bring many close but trust just only a few.

Remember, Judas had to be close to Jesus to be a Judas. If you are not close to someone, you can never be a Judas. A betrayer must always know things about you to give the information to the devil. He knows your schedule, where and when you pray, get up, and retreat. That is why it wasn't hard for the soldiers to find Jesus in the garden when they were looking for Him. Judas knew exactly where He was and what He was doing at that particular time. Audit your inner circle well and protect it from betrayers who will gossip and reveal information about you.

Become a person of few words.

"My dear brothers and sisters, take note of this: Everyone should be quick to listen, slow to speak and slow to become angry" (James 1:19 NIV). Don't be loose with your lips. Avoid people knowing your business. When someone knows so much about you, you give them the power to harm or use information against you. In my birth country, a traditional proverb says, "Those who say nothing at all never regret. But those who say too much will always have a lot to regret." In other words, those who keep silent never regret doing so. If there's nothing you say, there will be nothing to discuss or transfer to other people with additions or misconceptions.

Likewise, don't respond to everything people say to you. Sometimes, simply say, "I have heard, and let's pray about it." Often, people reveal the side of the story that makes them look bad. Gossipers never tell their side of the story, but they will tell another person's side. Some are so wicked that they always say what they were told but never what they said or contributed to the conversation. That is how ministries are polluted, contaminated, and misaligned, so be a person who speaks few words.

Pray.

As you engage in this battle to become a person of few words, handle it with prayer. James said, "If anyone among you thinks he is religious, and does not bridle his tongue but deceives his own heart, this one's religion *is* useless" (James 1:26), and "If anyone does not stumble in word, he *is* a perfect man, able also to bridle the whole body" (James 3:2). In prayer, you can ask the Lord to restrain your tongue from saying what you shouldn't say and help you to talk only when you should be talking. The tongue is one small object that doesn't have bones but can break very strong things. So, as small as it is, the tongue is a make-or-break object. James says it's untamable, but through prayer, you can ask God to take over your tongue. In that way, you will not say things you will regret.

Avoid lethal people.

As much as possible, keep away from lethal people in the ministry. Lethal people have venomous spirits, words, attitudes, and speech. They are poisonous. They always have something negative to say regardless of how someone tries. They always have bad comments and cannot say anything positive. Their only contribution is negativity. They are like the people described in Psalm 140:

> They sharpen their tongues like a serpent; The poison of asps *is* under their lips. *Selah* [4] Keep me, O LORD, from the hands of the wicked; Preserve me from violent men, Who have purposed to make my steps stumble. (Psalm 140:3-4 NKJV)

Stay away!

Expose gossip by bringing the involved parties face to face. Shed light on secrecy's darkness.

One of the best ways to drive gossip out of an organization or church is to hit it face on. I have learned that when someone says not to tell anyone, they simply mean let's see who will be the first one to tell because every information that goes beyond two people is no longer a secret. You must be very smart and wise. If the focus of the gossip is spreading and is a sensitive issue, it's better you call all the involved parties and ask them to repeat what so and so said behind your back in your face—in front of everyone. If you do that one or two times, the serpent of gossip will likely be beheaded.

If a church member brings you gossip, ask them if they can say it in front of whoever they are gossiping about. If they refuse, or they say they can't do it, know that it's not true—it is gossip. If a matter is true and you mean well, you should be able to say it in the ears of the responsible parties without fear. I know some people use the excuse of not being confrontational, but confrontational or not, you should be able to say what you have to say behind someone's back in their own hearing if it is true.

If you implement these solutions to confront gossip and hypocrisy, you will be positioned for victory in these battles. May God empower you, in Jesus' name.

Chapter 13: Jezebels

> But Jezebel his wife came to him, and said to him, "Why is your spirit so sullen that you eat no food?" ⁶ He said to her, "Because I spoke to Naboth the Jezreelite, and said to him, 'Give me your vineyard for money; or else, if it pleases you, I will give you *another* vineyard for it.' And he answered, 'I will not give you my vineyard.' " ⁷ Then Jezebel his wife said to him, "You now exercise authority over Israel! Arise, eat food, and let your heart be cheerful; I will give you the vineyard of Naboth the Jezreelite." (1 Kings 21:5-7 NKJV)

Jezebel was a Zidonian (or Sidonian) who served Baal and worshipped him (1 Kings 16:31). However, she married Ahab, king of Israel, primarily as a political arrangement to strengthen ties between the two kingdoms. So, she became a Baal and Ashtoreth-worshipping queen of Israel, God's chosen nation. Her lifestyle, gods, and corrupted nature contaminated the land. When Naboth would not give her husband, the king, his vineyard, Jezebel pointed out that the king was in authority—yet she would bypass that authority and get him what he wanted. The king had exercised enough protocol and restraint to ask Naboth—to humble himself even though he was a king and submit a request to Naboth. But not Jezebel. No, she resorted to treachery to get what she wanted. When Naboth refused the king's request,

Jezebel executed her own plot to take his vineyard. This is what she did:

> And she wrote letters in Ahab's name, sealed *them* with his seal, and sent the letters to the elders and the nobles who *were* dwelling in the city with Naboth. ⁹ She wrote in the letters, saying, Proclaim a fast, and seat Naboth with high honor among the people; ¹⁰ and seat two men, scoundrels, before him to bear witness against him, saying, "You have blasphemed God and the king." *Then* take him out, and stone him, that he may die. ¹¹ So the men of his city, the elders and nobles who were inhabitants of his city, did as Jezebel had sent to them, as it *was* written in the letters which she had sent to them. ¹² They proclaimed a fast, and seated Naboth with high honor among the people. ¹³ And two men, scoundrels, came in and sat before him; and the scoundrels witnessed against him, against Naboth, in the presence of the people, saying, "Naboth has blasphemed God and the king!" Then they took him outside the city and stoned him with stones, so that he died. ¹⁴ Then they sent to Jezebel, saying, "Naboth has been stoned and is dead." ¹⁵ And it came to pass, when Jezebel heard that Naboth had been stoned and was dead, that Jezebel said to Ahab, "Arise, take possession of the vineyard of Naboth the Jezreelite, which he refused to give you for money; for Naboth is not alive, but dead." ¹⁶ So it was, when Ahab heard that Naboth was dead, that Ahab got up and went down to take possession of the vineyard of Naboth the Jezreelite. (1 Kings 21:5-16 NKJV)

Jezebel lied, connived, manipulated, and killed over a mere vineyard. Many people think only women can operate under the spirit of Jezebel's influence, but this wicked spirit can use men and women alike. Its roots are not in gender but in a thirst for power and control. Today, people—male and female—in life and ministry follow this same mode of operation.

Naboth's murder reveals the characteristics of those who have the Jezebel spirit:

1. They usurp or exercise authority in the name of someone who won't stand up to them. They are controlling.

This is rebellion, which is the sin of witchcraft (1 Samuel 15:23). The first thing she did was write letters in her husband's name and seal them with his seal. She issued orders that did not come from the king.

> And she wrote letters in Ahab's name, sealed *them* with his seal, and sent the letters to the elders and the nobles who *were* dwelling in the city with Naboth. (1 Kings 21:8 NKJV)

This spirit thwarts authority. Those with a Jezebel spirit are close to authority yet usurp it to get what they want. It's their way or the highway. They are controlling.

2. They seize control because of proximity or closeness to installed authority.

Jezebel could not seize control of Israel until she married Ahab. So, before Jezebels can control, they must gain a leadership position or be close to someone with one. When they do, they introduce demonic ideas like Jezebel introduced Ahab to Baal worship. So, if you're in leadership, you must be careful what voices come to your ears and who draws close to you. That is when they use their influence to introduce ideas that lead to error.

Their suggestions may seem simple and harmless, but they can lead to destruction and have serious consequences. For example, they may suggest changing or reshuffling the leadership team in a ministry. As they influence you about who should be on the pulpit and who should not, you might be making life-changing decisions. A seemingly small thing like that can cost you heavily. For example, I have seen a man of God lose his ministry and the grace of God upon his life the day he changed his driver.

One of the first things Jezebels do when they come close is plant their evil children in the ministry. Remember, Ahtaliah was Jezebel's daughter. They may seem faithful and even better than others in the ministry, but that is how they begin to install their children in key leadership positions. So be careful about someone you install who immediately changes who should do what and who should be where. They are trying to install their children. Remember, Jezebel has children she has trained on how to commit sexual immortality to bring down a church and a servant of God. John the Revelator was instructed to write this about Jezebel, "Nevertheless, I have this against you: You tolerate that woman Jezebel, who calls herself a prophet. By her teaching, she misleads my servants into sexual immorality and the eating of food sacrificed to idols" (Revelation 2:20 NIV).

There are ladies in the church who follow this pattern, especially those who accept and acknowledge the leadership of a male pastor at the expense of dishonoring and disrespecting their wives. I define that as ministry madness and extremely Jezebelic. If you can't submit to a pastor's wife, then don't sit under that covering because it will not yield any good to you except curses. Hagar thought she could summit only to Abraham and disrespect Sarah, her mistress (master), because the lines had crossed, but it didn't work. The Angel of the Lord instructed her to go back and submit to Sarah. Many ladies in churches and ministries miss the mark here. They cross boundaries by disrespecting married women when marriage is to be honored (Hebrews 13:4).

3. They seize control through sexual immorality.

Some go to the extremes of offering their bodies to the pastor to gain favor, influence, and a say in the ministry. As they do so, if that pastor is married, he often looks down on his spouse. He focuses on the Jezebel in the ministry, a destiny destroyer. When this kind of influence is in control, Jezebel will give gifts and say things like, "I'm giving you this, but don't tell your spouse," which exposes a wicked motive behind the gift. That is very wrong and misleading in the body of Christ. If your gift is clean, why shouldn't the pastor's spouse know about it? Why do it behind closed doors? They do that to gain leverage.

When Jezebel lulls leadership into sexual immorality, they use it to control them. They will get some kind of evidence and use it for threats of breaking the marriage or exposure. For example, one of the so-called ushers escorted a man of God off the pulpit, and they went into a private room where they waited for the pastor to close the service. The lady usher told the pastor he needed a massage after such ministry. And she started helping him to take off his shoes and fan him to cool down. She seduced him, and they fell into sin. He was married, so she always used threats of telling the wife and putting pictures on the Internet to draw him back and into deeper sexual sin. Jezebel is manipulative and intimidating.

This pastor ended up in a spiritual prison and bondage for years until, one day, he resolved to come out. He told his family and church members of his errors. That is how he broke loose from Jezebel's grip. So many ministers are in that grip and have never figured a way out. They are praying for deliverance, which will not come automatically without taking a step to expose Jezebel. One way to break free if you have been contaminated by this spirit called Jezebel is to give up your pride and image and come clean. This is not very easy for many ministers or members to do.

Many are not delivered until they get caught or forcefully exposed.

However, that means they did not come out through repentance and may find themselves in it again. Because they got caught, they were forced to admit what happened but did not decide to break out. There's a lot of inner power in making that decision rather than waiting to be caught. There's a difference when you choose freedom over bondage. When someone makes that personal decision to come out of Jezebel's manipulations, it can be life-changing and yield lasting results.

Zacchaeus, the tax collector, decided to repent and reinstate whatever he stole. Nobody told him to do so; it was a personal conviction (Luke 19:8). This was bound to be an everlasting deliverance. There are so many in Jezebel's bondage and cage, but what matters is how you break out of the cage. I know some who broke out and were back there in a few months, years, or weeks. Be free from this kind of spirit by exposing the truth willingly. If circumstances force you out, you might find yourself back in Jezebel's arms after the drama is over.

4. They seize control through monetary and material gifts.

They use gifts, money, and influence of any kind. They use their offerings or tithes to control the man or woman of God. You find them buying expensive vehicles, and clothes, and giving enormous sums of money. But they do so with wicked motives of gaining control and influence over the leadership.

Many Jezebels use money and gifts to buy their way up or to get their way. So even if someone is faithfully giving large sums, please don't use that as a basis for choosing them for a leadership position. It's just a Jezebel scheme often used to get what they want or achieve their goals. Eventually, that so-called deceptive giving will stop after they get what they want.

My spiritual mother once told me about a woman who gave a thousand-dollar offering every Sunday. So, she had a few church members draw close to her to find out what she was doing for a living. They discovered she was a teacher, and we all know that teachers don't make that much to be able to give a thousand dollars every week. My spiritual mother started taking aside that offering and not depositing it.

A few months later, this lady demanded to see the senior pastor and only the senior pastor—among all the ministers. She claimed that only the senior pastor could solve her problem. When they tried to get her to see one of the other pastors, she insulted them and said she only wanted to—and must—see the senior pastor. She spoke disrespectfully because of the money she had given.

The moment my spiritual mother got involved, she became very disrespectful towards her. She began to say, "After all the money I have given. . ." My spiritual mother told her no amount of money would allow her to be so disrespectful or control the ministry, and if she wanted it back, they had it anyway. They gave it all back in the same envelopes she had used to give.

That is how this Jezebel was halted and unable to get to the man of God to achieve her mischievous agenda. The man of God survived because of the wisdom of his wife. Jezebel is a spirit and can operate through men, but it often works through female church members. And sometimes, it will take both the man and woman of God in a ministry to overcome this spirit. If one has compromised, then there is an open door that must be shut. You have to disconnect speedily to save your marriage or your home.

5. They deceive, plot, and connive to get what they want.

Jezebel orchestrated a scenario so that scoundrels could bear false witness against Naboth.

> She wrote in the letters, saying, Proclaim a fast, and seat Naboth with high honor among the people; ¹⁰ and seat two men, scoundrels, before him to bear witness against him, saying, "You have blasphemed God and the king." *Then* take him out, and stone him, that he may die. (1 Kings 21:9-10 NKJV)

Be careful; watch and pray. People are not always what they seem. Some church leaders and ministers orchestrate circumstances and use gossip or false witnesses to smear your reputation or set you up for removal or shame.

6. They murder the innocent and authentic.

Like it or not, Jezebel will be a member of your church, especially if there is a high-level prophetic anointing and grace in your ministry. If there's no prophet of fire, Jezebel will not come, so Jezebel is an announcement that there is a prophet of fire in your midst. It's one of the spirits the devil uses to thwart the prophetic purpose of God and highlight the fake instead of the authentic. This should be a common expectation in a ministry. Wherever there's a mighty servant of power, expect Jezebels to be present because they are the devil's weapon to destroy mighty prophetic voices.

> And two men, scoundrels, came in and sat before him; and the scoundrels witnessed against him, against Naboth, in the presence of the people, saying, "Naboth has blasphemed God and the king!" Then they took him outside the city and stoned him with stones, so that he died. ¹⁴ Then they sent to Jezebel, saying, "Naboth has been stoned and is dead." ¹⁵ And it came to pass, when Jezebel

> heard that Naboth had been stoned and was dead, that Jezebel said to Ahab, "Arise, take possession of the vineyard of Naboth the Jezreelite, which he refused to give you for money; for Naboth is not alive, but dead." ¹⁶ So it was, when Ahab heard that Naboth was dead, that Ahab got up and went down to take possession of the vineyard of Naboth the Jezreelite. (1 Kings 21:13-16 NKJV)

Jezebel is a killer of the authentic and replaces it with the fake. She killed innocent Naboth, vowed to kill Prophet Elijah, and replaced the prophets of God with the prophets of Baal.

> Now Ahab told Jezebel everything Elijah had done and how he had killed all the prophets with the sword. ² So Jezebel sent a messenger to Elijah to say, "May the gods deal with me, be it ever so severely, if by this time tomorrow I do not make your life like that of one of them." ³ Elijah was afraid and ran for his life. (1 Kings 19:1-3a NIV)

Jezebel hates people who hear from God and intimidates them, forcing them into caves. That's one way this spirit silences God's authentic voice in a ministry and highlights demonic voices. Jezebel is gifted. She can teach and lead and has a very intimidating voice. When she is given reign, the ministry ceases to hear the voice of God but hears demonic, strange voices.

This manifests when:

- Envy and a murderous spirit silence vessels who are true voices of God, and foolish, wicked people are given platforms
- Ministries replace the Bible with modern novels, and people don't read the Bible but prayer books and so-called novels

- Churches replace worship with entertainment
- People replace a godly dress code with an ungodly, so-called modern one in ministry

7. They involve others in their treacherous schemes.

Jezebel solicited the help of scoundrels, pulling them into her scheme. She also fathoms people in ungodly directions, so they lose the core values of the Bible. Through her influence, Ahab began to worship Baal and build altars for him.

> He not only considered it trivial to commit the sins of Jeroboam son of Nebat, but he also married Jezebel daughter of Ethbaal king of the Sidonians, and began to serve Baal and worship him. (1 Kings 16:31 NIV)

Hopefully, this list helps you identify Jezebel's operations and those around you who may carry this spirit. So, let's turn to solutions.

How to Overcome the Spirit of Jezebel in the Ministry

Be a leader that inquires about every single detail, small or great.

There is an expression, "The devil is in the details," and it is true when it comes to Jezebel. Be sure to ask the Lord for direction to avoid undue influence from Jezebelic forces. Ask God about even the smallest aspects of the ministry, or you'll find yourself opening the wrong doors. Before you hand anyone the "keys to the ministry," scan them spiritually—do a spiritual background check on them.

Don't easily trust people, no matter how on fire for God they may seem. Many people have conditional fire; they pray in tongues when they're near a brother they want to marry. But instead of focusing on someone's tongues, focus on their character before making decisions about marriage or the ministry. Remember, Jezebel is deceptive; she can pose as humble but be very conniving and crafty.

Practice privacy.

Protect your inner circle, and don't let people know too much about your personal life or important details about the ministry. Don't share things people should not know because they could be used to open you up to be approached and confronted by Jezebel. Surround yourself with people who have Obadiah's heart and spirit.

> And Ahab had summoned Obadiah, his palace administrator. (Obadiah was a devout believer in the LORD. ⁴ While Jezebel was killing off the LORD's prophets, Obadiah had taken a hundred prophets and hidden them in two caves, fifty in each, and had supplied them with food and water.) ⁵ Ahab had said to Obadiah, "Go through the land to all the springs and valleys. Maybe we can find some grass to keep the horses and mules alive so we will not have to kill any of our animals." (1 Kings 18:3-5 NIV)

Zip up; keep yourself from sexual sins.

Jezebel's quickest way to initiate you is through sexual immorality; you can see this in Revelation 2:20-23.

> Nevertheless, I have this against you: You tolerate that woman Jezebel, who calls herself a prophet. By her teaching she misleads my servants into sexual immorality and the eating of food sacrificed to idols. ²¹ I have given her time to repent of her immorality, but she is unwilling. ²² So

I will cast her on a bed of suffering, and I will make those who commit adultery with her suffer intensely, unless they repent of her ways. ²³ I will strike her children dead. Then all the churches will know that I am he who searches hearts and minds, and I will repay each of you according to your deeds. (Revelation 2:20-23 NIV)

One of the quickest ways to cooperate with Jezebel is to sleep around. She works with seduction. She works with uncleanness, ungodliness, and unholiness. So zip up; if you don't practice these things, you will not cooperate with Jezebel.

No wonder those who operate in this spirit love to dress in skimpy clothes. Seductive women like to paint themselves and put on unnecessary eyelashes. It's a mode of seduction; it's a Jezebelic tactic. Eyes are the window to the soul and a point of seduction. Men also do the same by showing off their chests and using too much cologne to get attention. It is good to smell good, but what is your motive deep within? Is it for everybody to smell you? Then, you might be operating with the spirit of Jezebel.

One of the ways Jezebel gets in is through people's dress code. Many ladies dress in clothes that should not be worn in public because they are looking for a way to seduce a man. If you are carrying the right spirit, there's no way you'd be comfortable dressing sexily in the house of worship. Sexy things are meant for the bedroom of married couples, not the pulpit.

God doesn't want you to dress in a sexy way; He already laid down His standard of modesty in Timothy's book. So, anything sexy or seductive in the house of worship is highly Jezebelic. Like it or not, those who make it a practice to wear revealing sexy clothes in God's house are carrying that wrong spirit. God wants us to reveal our hearts, not our bodies, in His house. Joel 2:13 says, "Rend your heart and not your garments. Return to the LORD your God, for he is gracious and compassionate, slow to anger and abounding in love, and he relents from sending calamity (NIV).

Having an appropriate dress code to overcome and not propagate Jezebel's seduction is vitally important. Don't allow indecency to take over the house of God. Nudity has never been godly. Just because it's acceptable in Hollywood doesn't mean it's acceptable in the house of God. Friendship with the world is enmity with Christ. When you develop a friendship with Hollywood and its dress code, that is enmity to the house of God because the government of heaven is in charge of the house of God. What God hates, the heavenly government hates and does not approve.

Always remember to be accountable to the Lord in everything you do. Keep in mind that if anyone causes the little ones to stumble, it's better to have a large stone around their necks (Matthew 18:6-7). Jezebel entices you to seduce others through your dress code. One day, you will be held accountable for the souls that didn't make it because of the people who stumbled along the way because of your dress code. They came to the house of God to worship but ended up lusting instead of worshipping. Though they drove their cars to worship, you became a hindrance and a stumbling block for them to enter the presence of Yahweh.

Walk in purity.

People make the mistake of confronting Jezebel without understanding that purity in the spirit is the prerequisite to taking her down. That is why Jezebel was not killed by Elijah, Gehazi, or Jehu; it was the eunuchs (sexually pure) that killed her.
You must be living in purity to kill Jezebel. That is why some who attack her are destroyed; they are not pure. They have been eating at her table and want to turn around and kill her. You cannot walk around in covenant with her children and her money in your

account and want to confront her. She will turn around and kill you.

We have seen so many become victims instead of victors because they are unclean and compromise with women who are Jezebel's champions in secret. She's already in them, and they are trying to kill their champion. Instead of killing her, they kill themselves because every Jezebelic food you eat is an initiation. So, trying to kill Jezebel when she's already in you is destiny suicide.

Jezebels are very hard-hearted and unrepentant. However much time God gives them to respond, they don't. They are very committed to their ministry of sexual immorality and deception.

To maintain purity, disconnect or break covenant with the people this spirit operates through. While Ahab was married to Jezebel, she had access to operate in Israel. Many people operating in a Jezebel spirit are not people you are married to, so this makes it easier to break ties with them.

Avoid eating from Jezebel's table.

Do not take her gifts, which are weapons of deception and manipulation.

> Now summon the people from all over Israel to meet me on Mount Carmel. And bring the four hundred and fifty prophets of Baal and the four hundred prophets of Asherah, who eat at Jezebel's table." (1 Kings 18:19 NIV)

You'll eventually bow to Jezebel when you eat from her table. A Jezebelic person's reasons for funding and supporting the ministry are never authentic. They are doing so to contaminate or pollute the ministry. So, if you eat from her table, you will bow.

God told Elijah he had 7,000 who had not bowed to Jezebel. 1 Kings 19:18 says, "Yet I have left me seven thousand in Israel, all the knees which have not bowed unto Baal, and every mouth which hath not kissed him" (KJV). Every time we eat from her table or take her gifts, we kiss Jezebel and ingest her purposes. That is how we find ourselves fulfilling a demonic mandate instead of a godly one.

Behind every Jezebel is a devil, not an angel. So, there is no way Jezebel can fund your ministry, and you fulfill a divine mandate. One way or another, you will have to bow to her gods and kiss them, and one of her gods is Baal.

Avoid taking gifts because they will put you in a position to succumb to Jezebel's ideas. Do not allow yourself to be corrupted by gifts. Don't encourage that because the enemy is trying to purchase your soul or the ministry.

So, if you don't want to operate in or be a part of the Jezebelic system, stop taking her gifts and eating from her table. I know times may be hard, but refuse to feast and eat from the hands of Jezebel. The minute you eat food or get Jezebelic money, you are bound to become Jezebelic one way or another. It's a matter of time because the food you eat physically affects who you are spiritually.

If you eat vegetables without taking any proteins, you're bound to suffer nutritional problems or an unbalanced diet. So, to protect yourself from Jezebel, don't eat her food. I have seen people who say, "Oh, I'm strong." But it's a law of nature that what you feed your spirit with is what you'll produce. You can't plant a banana and expect to reap a mango or apple.

Operate in and walk in the light, which means walking in the truth always.

The opposite of truth is deception, which is Jezebel's trusted weapon. Let the Spirit of Truth be in you. That is the Spirit of God. Jezebel and the Spirit of God cannot operate in the same container or person. One has to take over; no two gods can abide in the same tabernacle. One way to thwart Jezebel is to bring back the truth.

Walk in the truth and train your members to walk in the truth. If you don't, Jezebel will teach them how to tell lies.

Walk in wisdom.

The Bible tells us to be as wise as serpents and harmless as doves (Matthew 10:16). It takes high-level wisdom to overcome Jezebel because, as we know, she is crafty and conniving. For example, Elijah knew Jezebel was there for the longest time but never confronted her. But when the divine revelation came, and God instructed him to show himself to Ahab, he was ready to confront her.

As a Christian, know when to hide, confront, or showcase yourself. We have lost many to Jezebel because instead of hiding, they were confronting. You need to know when to move to navigate against Jezebel.

Wait upon the Lord for direction and the right timing. What you're doing may be good, but is it the right time? The whole time before Elijah appeared before Ahab, he was being empowered to face Jezebel.
Elijah had the strength to execute all the prophets of Baal who ministered at the altars that empowered Jezebel. Now, with all her prophets dead, Jezebel was too weak. That is why when she heard that Elijah had killed the prophets, she swore to kill him. Her power base had been destroyed. It was just a matter of time before she was killed.

Chapter 14: Loneliness

"Look and see, there is no one at my right hand; no one is concerned for me. I have no refuge; no one cares for my life." – King David in Psalm 142:4 NIV

David wrote this psalm while hiding in the Cave of Adullam from his enemies.[3] Pastors' wives can relate. Sometimes, they are surrounded by church members yet feel they have no one they can confide in who truly cares for their lives. In fact, many pastors' wives have what I define as loneliness syndrome. This is when an individual lacks a companion to confide in and share personal or secretive matters. Although they are surrounded by many people, it does not mean they can trust them with their innermost issues and circumstances. Perhaps you can relate? I encourage husband-pastors to read this chapter with their wives.

As a pastor's wife, you may often have no one to open up to wholeheartedly because of the fear of exposure and backlash. There's no one you can safely "undress" in front of emotionally, and everyone needs such people to share their innermost issues with without feeling judged or ashamed because everyone has silent frustrations. Many women suffer inwardly when such

---

[3] Matthew Henry, "Commentary on Psalm 142," Blue Letter Bible. Accessed October 7, 2024, https://www.blueletterbible.org/Comm/mhc/Psa/Psa_142.cfm.

things are not shared or addressed with a confidant. This has contributed to the number of pastor's wives and church leaders that are suffering from ailments such as depression, high blood pressure, and trauma.

Most pastors' wives hide their loneliness and frustration because everyone sees them as an embodiment of strength, direction, stability, and hope. They are afraid to share their personal challenges, which eventually causes them to drown and not swim through life's challenges. It is okay that challenges are there, but you die in them if you can't swim through them.

Loneliness is a great battle that every pastor's wife will face at one point or another, so you must know what to do and where to run to get help. I've seen some go to counselors whom they don't know or talk to people on the phone who cannot see them because they're afraid to reveal their identity. They don't want to reveal who they are because they have a husband and family, but they cannot open up to them because they want them to look at them with respect and dignity.

Sometimes, when you open up to people about your pains and challenges, they respond with disrespect, which no pastor's wife enjoys. Because everyone expects you to be superhuman, you may lose respect before the people you lead. That can be humiliating because, most of the time, you are looked at as a great success. People view you like a fantasy or celebrity, and any attempt to reveal anything different can cause them to criticize or disrespect you.

So, most pastors' wives smile just to keep up appearances; they "grin and bear it." However, on the inside, they are in great pain and agony they can never share—not even with family. This reminds me vividly of a pastor's wife, who I admired greatly. I thought everything about her and her marriage was perfect.

Believe me, that is what was portrayed outwardly.

During one of our prayer retreats, she happened to share with me. She said, "Beloved, if I was to open up to you and show you the wounds in my heart, you would run and faint." It was clear that this pastor's wife was battered on the inside but had to put up a picture of great strength because of her love for God and to hold the ministry together. She died suddenly, only a few months after sharing her pain with me.

The wounds she had hidden for so long, covered so well, and carried around graciously had killed her. No one could smell her wounds oozing or detect her internal emotional bleeding. It was taking a toll on her life, but she had no one to trust with her pain. Even though she had a husband who everyone looked at as a great pastor. She died suddenly without sickness or warning.

Sadly, so many pastors' wives are in a similar situation. They are leading while bleeding because of loneliness. Bleeding in ministry is okay, but not having someone to help control it can be detrimental. Scientifically, when you bleed continuously, you lose life. This explains why many pastors' wives who were on fire have become lifeless and disinterested in ministry. Ministry, which was once a joy and passion, has now become a big burden. This is a sign of spiritual deprivation or burnout due to loneliness and depression.

People often don't suspect a pastor's wife to be lonely. Why would a leader with a husband and family be lonely? That would be the first question someone could ask. However, many busy pastors don't make time with their spouses a priority. One of her most common battles is getting her husband to strike a balance between ministry, marriage, and family. I want to submit to every married person that after your relationship with God and spending time with Him, your priority should be spending time with your spouse.

There is a battle between a woman and God for the heart of her pastor-husband. Every woman wants the heart of her husband, but God also wants a man's heart. That's why God had great consideration for David even when he sinned—he was a man after God's heart. He was loved by God and favored like no other because his heart was after God.

Many pastors' wives are married but actually single because they never spend time with their spouses. They never see them. They have different sets of friends and programs. The only time they come together is when they are going to church. Other than that, they lead separate, private lives. They only look like they're married when they sit together in the front row at church. They never pray together. Their husband is busy praying for and ministering to others but never to them. Such pastors' wives who don't have a solid foundation in Christ can engage in many things to cover their pain.

Focus on your bride.

Husband-pastor, we are living in an era and a generation where many pastors have forgotten that the church is the bride of Christ, and their bride is their wife. They have taken their focus off their wives and put it on Christ's bride, the church. This is a total misunderstanding and misplacement of interests. It is like taking your interest and focus off your own wife and putting it on someone else's wife. That abomination should be addressed to save pastors' homes and marriages. This should be priority number one—not second or third.

Likely, some men and women of God will not make it to heaven because of the errors they made in their marriages. When interviewed during the last years of their ministry, many of God's generals said they wished they had spent more time with their families. It's very important for servants of God not to mix up their priorities. It is dangerous to consider ministry more important than your marriage, wife, and children. Let's get our priorities right so we can get the Kingdom's priorities right. If we get one wrong, everything is going to be wrong, distorted, and out of order.

Very few servants of God have overcome this crisis in their homes. Pastors are always busy seeking God, counseling others, or praying for church members. They are busy with ministerial engagements and church administration. They rarely spend time with their children, much less their wives, so they are more devoted to the ministry and God than their wives. The wives feel left out with no one to turn to. This is a problem of failing to find balance.

This failure causes pastors' wives to suffer from emotional and attention deficiency. They feel so alone. Once this is not controlled or addressed in a timely manner, physical, emotional, and spiritual ailments begin to emerge. To avoid grievous consequences, pastors should help their wives not to fall into the snare of depression, which is one of the main catalysts for severe mental health issues. Everyone deserves to feel loved, respected, given attention, and cared for, so let's discuss ways to win the battle against loneliness.

Solutions: Winning the Battle Against Loneliness

Develop a very strong personal relationship with the Holy Spirit.

He is the best comforter. He can even comfort you when your husband cannot and strengthen you when you have no might. When you're in constant fellowship with the Holy Spirit, the joy of the Lord will strengthen you in life's journey. Nehemiah wrote,

"The joy of the Lord is your strength" (Nehemiah 8:10).

Know that your husband is not your source of strength, but God is the source of your life, ministry, and calling so that when your pastor-husband does not give you attention or what you need as a woman in ministry, you do not give up. It is very important to have the Holy Spirit breathe on you every single day of your life. He will help you overlook many things that could cause frustration and see them as vanity, as Solomon wrote (Ecclesiastes 1:1).

Have a spiritual covering or mentor to whom you can "undress" emotionally.

You must have someone you can "undress" to emotionally or spiritually without feeling judged. Sometimes, all someone needs is to be listened to or given an ear. This is a great healing to the soul and spirit. That is why when someone is grieving the loss of a loved one, they are encouraged to cry and let their emotions out. You don't stop the tears until the pain ceases. Releasing the pressure and the tension inside us is a great relief to our souls; it's the door to inner healing. That's why it's important to have a listening ear when you're going through the valley of certain issues in life.

I pray that every pastor's wife will find someone they can undress to emotionally and not feel ashamed or judged. This eases a lot of tension and pain and restores the inner peace and calmness that is necessary to thrive in life.

Let the Word of God strengthen you.

Loneliness can also be overcome by strengthening yourself in the Word of God. David faced loneliness and encouraged himself in the Lord. He did not wait for anyone to come and prop him up. 1

Samuel 30:6 says, "But David encouraged himself in the LORD his God" (KJV).

As a daughter in Zion, you must learn to encourage yourself in the Lord through worship, praise, and, most importantly, the Word of God. Anytime God uses someone mightily, they will experience loneliness at some point. It comes with the territory called ministry.

This happened to Elijah when he said, "I am the only one" (1 Kings 19:10). He felt alone, but the fact was he was not alone because God said he had 7,000 prophets who had not kissed Baal (1 Kings 19:18). So, there are many children of God who feel alone, but in actual sense, they are not. I pray that God will show you your DNA and lineage in the spirit so you can align yourself with the truth that you are not alone and not succumb to the battle with loneliness.

If pastors' wives continue on the path of loneliness, they will make decisions that are detrimental to their husbands and the ministry. I know a pastor's wife who woke up one morning and filed for divorce—it was a surprise to everyone. She was sick and tired and tired of being sick and tired as well. Pastors, help your wives not to lose their minds because, for some, it was you who dragged them into ministry. They didn't have such plans or agendas.

Ground yourself in the Word of God and note how those in the Scriptures handled loneliness. What does the Bible say about loneliness?

> Turn to me and have mercy, for I am alone and in deep distress. (Psalm 25:16 NLT)

> Look and see, there is no one at my right hand; no one is concerned for me. I have no refuge; no one cares for my life. [5] I cry to you, LORD; I say, "You are my refuge, my

portion in the land of the living." (Psalm 142:4-5 NIV)

Fear not, for I *am* with you; Be not dismayed, for I *am* your God. I will strengthen you, Yes, I will help you, I will uphold you with My righteous right hand.' (Isaiah 41:10 NKJV)

Give all your worries and cares to God, for he cares about you. (1 Peter 5:7 NLT)

Strike a balance between ministry and family.

Because many pastors fail to balance their home life, marriage, and children with the ministry and other engagements, their homes are in crisis. This has caused a lot of imbalances and deficiencies in pastoral homes.

That's why I want to remind every man of God that the same God who called you and gave you a ministry also told you to love your wife and gave you your children. He's expecting you to succeed at everything He has entrusted to you.

Instead of prioritizing other things, come back to the center of it all and get your priorities in divine order. It is God first, next your wife, then family, and after them, the ministry. Some people do not agree, but let me explain. If this order is distorted, everything else will also be distorted; it will be out of order.

I've heard people say God first, then your ministry, your wife and children last. This is not biblical. It is just a hyper-spiritual doctrine that has destroyed many homes, families, and ministries.

The church that you give preeminence over your wife is the bride of Christ. Your bride is your wife. Every time you take your eyes off your own bride and focus on Christ's bride more than your own, you fall out of alignment. God will also come and fight you because He is jealous of His bride.

The church has never been your bride—the church is the bride of Christ. I want you to imagine a situation where somebody comes and tries to take your place in your wife's life. Will you keep quiet and look on? As far as I know, men cannot stand this—born-again or not. They rise up in jealousy and fight that man with every fiber of their beings to ensure he leaves their wife alone.

I want to submit that some pastors are at war with God because they are trying to take the bride of Christ as their own. So, it's not demons fighting you. Christ Himself has come against you because you're trying to own and possess what He has not given you to own and possess. So, as much as you are a man of God, be sure not to think you own the church or the ministry. The parable in Matthew 21 sheds light on this:

> "Hear another parable: There was a certain landowner who planted a vineyard and set a hedge around it, dug a winepress in it and built a tower. And he leased it to vinedressers and went into a far country. 34 Now when vintage-time drew near, he sent his servants to the vinedressers, that they might receive its fruit. 35 And the vinedressers took his servants, beat one, killed one, and stoned another. 36 Again he sent other servants, more than the first, and they did likewise to them. 37 Then last of all he sent his son to them, saying, 'They will respect my son.' 38 But when the vinedressers saw the son, they said among themselves, 'This is the heir. Come, let us kill him and seize his inheritance.' 39 So they took him and cast *him* out of the vineyard and killed *him*. 40 "Therefore, when the owner of the vineyard comes, what will he do to those vinedressers?" 41 They said to Him, "He will destroy those wicked men miserably, and

lease *his* vineyard to other vinedressers who will render to him the fruits in their seasons." (Matthew 21:33-41 NKJV)

The vinedressers in this parable are the ministers or pastors entrusted with the vineyard, but the Lord is the landowner. God did not give you the vineyard as a permanent owner. He just leased it to you.

In the parable, people fought every time God sent someone to the vineyard because they had a misconception that the vineyard belonged to them—no, they were just vinedressers who had been hired (leased). God did not give it to them. When the son was sent, it represented how Christ was killed. So, you become replaceable whenever you do not represent God well in the vineyard. Most pastors have tried to take God's place and abandoned their places in their homes and marriages. Being a pastor does not make you a God. There is only one savior of men, Jesus Christ our Lord.

> Jesus said to them, "Have you never read in the Scriptures: 'The stone which the builders rejected Has become the chief cornerstone. This was the LORD's doing, And it is marvelous in our eyes'? [43] "Therefore I say to you, the kingdom of God will be taken from you and given to a nation bearing the fruits of it. [44] And whoever falls on this stone will be broken; but on whomever it falls, it will grind him to powder." (Matthew 21:42-43 NKJV)

The Kingdom of God will be taken from you and given to a nation that will bear fruit. So, before you take ministry so seriously, take your wife seriously. She's your bride—not the church. Once you align yourself properly with the Kingdom's order, some battles will cease in your ministry. Some battles are there because you are trying to take Christ's bride to be your own bride. If pastors fix this, God will be at peace with them, and there'll be a revival in the house of God again.

Paul even said if you don't treat your wife well, your prayers will be hindered (1 Peter 3:7). However anointed a man of God may be, some things will only be rendered to you by God *if your wife approves and is in agreement with you*. Many pastors overlook their wives, but just because you overlook her doesn't mean God does. That is why in the days of Abraham, when Sarah cast out Hagar and Abraham did not like it, as anointed and powerful as Abraham was, God commanded him to listen to his wife (Genesis 21:12).

Pastors, one of the ways to please God and have ministry moving in the best direction for you is to love your wife as Christ loved the church. Many pastors have things moving in the opposite direction in ministry because of the error of abandoning their wives and not even providing for them. But they provide for the church. Hypothetically speaking, it doesn't make sense when you dress up someone else's bride, give them all the jewelry and all they need, and do not take care of your bride. In modern-day Christianity, this would be deemed as madness of the highest order.

If I may pose a question, based on the church being Christ's bride, do you think some pastors are operating in madness or the anointing? Especially consider those who can foot all the church bills but never have money to pay for their wives' nails, hairdos, vacations, or whatever small things make them happy. So, some things look spiritual and godly, but they are *not* biblical.

Stay in divine order.

When you stay in divine order, it strengthens your authority in the realm of the spirit. Because it's illegal to operate under the authority of God when you are not under authority. You're out of order when you're not in divine alignment with your wife or husband. Therefore, you don't have a legitimate standing in the spirit. Demons can challenge you whenever you pray or fast because you have an open door.

God wants every pastor's house to be in order rather than out of order. Remember, pastors are lawmakers and spiritual litigators. It's important that litigators also keep the laws they make and live exemplary lives for others.

After you distort divine order, you become a lawbreaker in the realm of the spirit. Lawbreakers cannot become kingdom builders. How many criminals become prominent leaders in our society? That is highly unlikely, and if it's highly unlikely in the natural realm, then it's also highly unlikely in the spiritual realm.

So, husband-pastors, pay attention to your wife's needs. It is godly when you spend time with your wife and children in the house instead of locking yourself up in the room to spend time in the Word and prayer every time you're home. I know a man who calls himself super-spiritual. Whenever he gets home, he locks himself up and says he's praying. The wife has become both a father and a mother to the children because their daddy is always praying and reading the Word. This pastor is very confused.

God designed families to be raised by both mothers and fathers. When you leave your responsibility to your wife, you have distorted God's order, and this will be detrimental not only to your children but also to the ministry, whether you like it or not. A minister produces after his own kind. You will find yourself with so-called strong spirituality and a broken home.

God will hold you accountable for having a broken home. Many pastors will find themselves in hell because of the way they treated their wives, who are daughters of Zion. Every time you trespass against your wife and shut them down in the name of submission, you are committing sin against their Father, God almighty.

As a biological father, would you be happy with a man who marries your daughter but treats her like garbage? I believe you wouldn't, so what makes you think that when you maltreat a daughter of Zion, God is going to keep celebrating, using, and blessing you? Consider the answer in this passage of Scripture:

> And this is the second thing you do: You cover the altar of the LORD with tears, With weeping and crying; So He does not regard the offering anymore, Nor receive *it* with goodwill from your hands. [14] Yet you say, "For what reason?" Because the LORD has been witness Between you and the wife of your youth, With whom you have dealt treacherously; Yet she is your companion And your wife by covenant. (Malachi 2:13-14 NKJV)

In this Scripture, God is no longer receiving offerings from his hands nor listening to the cry of this weeping man. Though he kept asking God why, God's answer was that he had dealt treacherously with the wife of his youth. Many pastors have battered their wives emotionally and spiritually, and they have lost their self-esteem. They cannot tell you anything. If they try to, you make them feel like you did them a favor by marrying them because, lately, marrying a pastor looks like it gives you status in society.

However, I want to remind you that your wife was not looking for status when she married you. Social media makes it easy to have status. But when your wife said, "I do," they were looking for a husband, not social status. Many pastors in the modern-day church have demeaned their wives, and it is crazy for them to think God cannot see what they are doing behind the scenes.

Some of them have gone to the extent of boasting to their wives that many women in the church want them. Some have gone further and turned their spiritual daughters into sexual amenities. They look at their wives as nothing because many of the Jezebelic women in the ministry can afford to buy them new cars, and suits, and fund TV programs and conferences. They feed the pastor's ego, but their wife only feeds their spirit, so their husbands further demean them.

So many men enjoy their ego being fed, but after it's fed and is so big, where will it lead you? To heaven or to hell? The last time I checked, many egotistic men did not go to heaven but instead to hell because they sought their way and not God's way. Ego will lead you into a way that seems right to every man, but its end is destruction. As we all know, man's ways are not God's ways.

Men of God, be careful with anyone who feeds your ego, and be very protective and loving to the people who feed your spirit, especially your wife. She is the one who is bold enough to tell you when you are wrong or even possibly warn you about pending destruction. Sometimes, pastors take offense at this and don't even want to come near their wives because they are always telling them what they are not doing right. However, always remember that correction is what makes you a better man, preacher, husband, and father.

Be humble before God. When your ego is fed more than your spirit, you will produce the fruits of pride; but when your spirit man is fed, you will produce humility, submission, and meekness, which enables us to inherit the earth (Matthew 5:5). Meekness will give you spiritual possessions in the earth realm and the reverse is true. A lack of meekness will deny you the acquisition of your earthly blessings or possessions. Pastors, be mindful of this.

I want you to remember that God can watch you disrespect and dishonor your wife. He observes this treacherous behavior towards your wife. If you continue, every time you lift up your hands to pray, your hands are stained. God cannot use such hands. If you want God to hear your prayer and your cry again, return to divine alignment and order with your wife.

Chapter 15: Rebellious Children

"Correct your son, and he will give you rest; Yes, he will give delight to your soul." – Solomon in Proverbs 29:17 NKJV

Most pastors and pastors' wives dream of seeing their children do well in life, serve the Lord gladly, and even follow in their footsteps in ministry. However, because the devil targets pastors and their children, that dream is sometimes shattered, and they face the battle of rebellious children. When they do, their children's behavior quickly becomes the subject of church gossip, and the pressure mounts to see their children change for the better.

Undoubtedly, this creates stress in many ways. If pastors and pastors' wives facing this battle are not strong, they can begin to question their calling or feel guilty because of what the Scriptures say in 1 Timothy 3:

> Now the overseer is to be above reproach . . . [4] He must manage his own family well and see that his children obey him, and he must do so in a manner worthy of full respect. [5] (If anyone does not know how to manage his own family, how can he take care of God's church?) (1 Timothy 3:1,4-5 NIV)

Knowing your children are walking in rebellion can shatter your confidence because having them in order is one of the biblical expectations of a church leader. However, several leaders in the Bible went through this battle, including David, a man after God's heart, and Eli, a head priest. So, no pastor's wife should think it's strange if they find themselves fighting this battle.

Indeed, pastor's wife, I want you to know that some children rebel against the vision and faith of their parents no matter how holy and upright their parents may be. The pivotal factor is that you continue to correct, warn, and instruct your children in the ways of the Lord—no matter what. Whether it looks like they are listening or not, you must continue to teach what is right to ensure you remain faithful in God's eyes when they are not faithful.

Eli provides an object lesson related to this truth. He was the head priest at Shiloh who observed Hannah as she poured out her heart to God, asking for a child. Eli blessed her and told her God would give her a son, and He did. She gave birth to Samuel, who would later become a great prophet. In return, she kept her vow to give the child back to the Lord to serve Him. Samuel became an apprentice under Eli. Hannah and her husband would return to Shiloh each year to worship and check on their son. Each time they did, Eli would pronounce a blessing over them and say, "The LORD give you descendants from this woman for the loan that was given to the LORD." Then they would go to their own home." (1 Samuel 2:20 NKJV). The loan was, of course, giving Samuel back to the Lord.

But while Eli was busy training young Samuel and blessing others, as so many pastors are busy doing, his sons were working evil. Eli's sons were young priests under his charge, responsible for the offerings in the temple at Shiloh. But the Scriptures say they were rebellious. "Now the sons of Eli *were* corrupt; they did not know the LORD" (1 Samuel 2:12 NKJV). So it is possible for a parent to be upright and know the ways of God, but their children not know God.

Eli is a powerful priest who can be seen as a modern-day pastor, but his children were not restrained early enough. As a result, they did not align with the priestly vision or call upon the family. This ended in judgment not only on the family but also on the entire nation because the glory of God departed or lifted. "Therefore the sin of the young men was very great before the LORD, for men abhorred the offering of the LORD" (1 Samuel 2:17 NKJV).

Eli was very old before he understood the magnitude of his son's evil. Pastor's wife, restrain your children early.

> Now Eli was very old; and he heard everything his sons did to all Israel, and how they lay with the women who assembled at the door of the tabernacle of meeting. 23 So he said to them, "Why do you do such things? For I hear of your evil dealings from all the people. 24 No, my sons! For *it is* not a good report that I hear. You make the LORD's people transgress. 25 If one man sins against another, God will judge him. But if a man sins against the LORD, who will intercede for him?" Nevertheless they did not heed the voice of their father, because the LORD desired to kill them. (1 Samuel 2:22-25 NKJV)

This was an extreme situation. Eli's son's wickedness was so severe that God wanted to kill them. Eli could have restrained them before it reached that point, but he was busy ministering to others. Even so, once he tried to correct them, they would not listen. God saw that they would not repent or relent from defiling His temple and determined His own course of action to bring their deeds to an end.

Submissive Spiritual Children vs. Rebellious Biological Children

Hannah's son, Samuel, was under Eli's tutelage and the exact opposite of Eli's sons. "Samuel ministered before the LORD, *even as* a child, wearing a linen ephod" (1 Samuel 2:18 NKJV). While God had taken a decision to punish Eli's biological sons, his spiritual son, Samuel, "grew in stature, and in favor both with the LORD and men" (1 Samuel 2:26 NKJV).

This is another common battle pastor's wives confront. They have submissive spiritual children, but their own children refuse to submit. A primary reason for this dilemma is familiarity. Pastors' children become so familiar with their parents' flaws and shortcomings in the house that they don't respect their heavenly callings and ministries.

Children are very familiar with their parents' voices and characters. Besides your spouse, they are the first to see your weaknesses, which may be a temper like Moses, lack of faith under threatenings, like Elijah, or fear of persecution like Peter, who denied Christ thrice, or your manner of relating to your spouse. Once they identify weaknesses in your walk with God, they may not have the understanding or revelation to be able to continue to respect you.

Children who walk in familiarity often have trouble safeguarding their parents' nakedness. Noah went through a similar experience.

> Noah, a man of the soil, proceeded to plant a vineyard. [21] When he drank some of its wine, he became drunk and lay uncovered inside his tent. [22] Ham, the father of Canaan, saw his father naked and told his two brothers outside. [23] But Shem and Japheth took a garment and laid it across their shoulders; then they walked in backward and

covered their father's naked body. Their faces were turned the other way so that they would not see their father naked. ²⁴ When Noah awoke from his wine and found out what his youngest son had done to him, ²⁵ he said, "Cursed be Canaan! The lowest of slaves will he be to his brothers." (Genesis 9:20-25 NIV)

Ham, the father of Canaan, saw his father's nakedness and spread the news to his brothers. Instead of Shem and Japheth running to see their father exposed, they walked backward to cover his nakedness. Ham represents pastors' children who, because of their parents' private lives or weaknesses, find it difficult to cover and respect them. They find it difficult to believe in their God, to trust them, and to view them as spiritual authorities.

Familiarity and Rebellion

Children see the private lives of their pastor-parents that others don't see, which causes familiarity. As the saying goes, "familiarity breeds contempt," and contempt brings rebellion. "Rebellion is as the sin of witchcraft, and stubbornness is as iniquity and idolatry. Because thou hast rejected the word of the LORD, he hath also rejected thee from being king" (1 Samuel 15:23 KJV).

How can you see your father or mother and, at the same time, look at them as your pastor, prophet, or mentor? Regardless of how heavy and strong the anointing someone carries, they are still flesh and blood. They can err. The Bible says in the book of James that Elijah was a man of passion, just like us. The anointing doesn't make us any different. We still have the human element or human factor in us. We can go wrong.

However, we can also be corrected if we are teachable and have the right people to do checks and balances in our lives. That is an example we should model for our children. So many pastors and their wives have continued in error, which has endangered the upcoming generation. Still, that doesn't give rebellious children the authority or legality to doubt the existence of God or the spiritual authority their parents hold.

Respect is reverence or honor and a very important factor. Familiarity can cause a lack of respect. If you don't respect somebody, you will rebel against them. I can issue a command, and someone responds to it or obeys it because they respect my authority. But once they don't respect my authority, they will live in disobedience.

Shem and Japheth understood the rules of respect and authority. They covered their father, refusing to fix their eyes on his state of weakness but rather maintain their honor for him. They remained blessed while Noah cursed Ham and Canaan. That's the difference between pastors' children who refuse to become familiar with and dishonor their parents no matter what and those who despise their parents' weaknesses—blessings and curses.

So, how do we bring a balance? Or how do we achieve the same thing we achieve spiritually with our biological children?

Solutions for Winning the Battle of Rebellious Children

Be a Christian in private and public.

Don't have two faces or two sets of character traits. Don't have a different public version of yourself than your private life because we all know some people living double lives. They are different in public than in private. Their children can see the habits that bind them. Some are drinking alcohol, living in adultery, and have unaddressed character flaws that trigger their children's rebellion. The best way to stop that is to have integrity.

Have one face, and let that face be that of Christ. And when we talk about character, match your character to the character of Christ. That is how you can avoid rebellion. Lead by example. As Paul said, "Follow me as I follow Christ" (1 Corinthians 11:1 KJV).

Don't hesitate to discipline your children.

Biological and spiritual children all err, sin, or fall into deception, which leads to rebellion. At some point, Satan is going to tempt them to rebel or walk in disrespect, but you should never hold back the rod of correction. The Bible says, "Whoever spares the rod hates their children, but the one who loves their children is careful to discipline them" (Proverbs 13:24 NIV). So, wherever rebellion is exhibited, you must stand up and cut it off immediately.

Discipline for Spiritual versus Biological Children

When spiritual children misbehave or if you notice they have a character flaw, you need to discipline them. They may be good ministers or gifted, but don't let them continue because of their gift. For their gift to profit the generation or have longevity, you need to discipline them. If you discipline them, you'll be pruning the gift and making them better. Do not hesitate to give correction, tell them to sit down, or not serve again until that character issue is fixed.

Lack of spiritual discipline is why we have two breeds of Christians in the church today. There are Christians who are truly Christians. There are also so-called "Christians" who are only Christians for the sake of their service to the church.

A primary example is very gifted keyboard players, but they are out of order and out of character. They come to church only for their paycheck and don't even receive the Word of God. The pastor is afraid to correct them because they are gifted. They hold back the discipline. They say, "Oh, just keep on playing. You're the only one available." However, we cannot keep on offering strange fires to God. If the keyboard player is defiled, have the audacity and the boldness to address it. Tell them that for the next month or the next year, don't play the keyboard until you are fixed in this area. Because as much as they are gifted, whatever they are offering unto God is not even truly worship.

We have to discipline spiritual and biological children spiritually and physically. Eli failed to restrain his sons, and the sin of rebellion brought judgment upon him, the house of God, and then the entirety of Israel (and the Bible says the voice of God was scarce in Israel). As pastors' wives and pastors, we are responsible for restraining our children. When we don't train and discipline them, we are not offering God true worship.

We must be intentional and vigilant in disciplining our children because the next generation is at stake. People may think you're extreme, and so may your children. They may complain, but, in the end, it will benefit them. For example, some people consider the African way of disciplining children extreme, but their heart is right. They just want their children to turn out right.

To bring balance, try having someone speak to your children. There's a rising trend nowadays where pastors' children are having conferences where they talk through certain issues unique to preachers' kids. Talking through these things helps them not transgress against their parents' anointing.

Even if your biological child transgresses against God's anointing, it will damage them. You can see that with Noah. The anointing damaged Noah's children, and one of them came out with curses. Noah's children also experienced judgment when they messed with an anointed man. So, the boundaries have to be explained.

They have to know that even though they are your biological child, they have to understand that the hand of the Lord rests upon you. When they hurt you, the Lord is not pleased with them. If they become an enemy to you, they become an enemy to the Lord. They need that training and teaching.

They need help in this area to protect you and them. They cannot only see you as their mother. They must see the grace, office, and ministry to which God called you, and there are boundaries they cannot cross with you. They need people to help them draw the boundary line because as much as they are your biological child, that doesn't exempt them from the judgment of God.

Help your children avoid rebellion by having people train, teach, and admonish them not to be familiar with or hold their parents in contempt—regardless of the flaws they see. Teach them how to respect the anointing and the anointed.

Every child and family is different. People have different disciplinary measures that work for them. What works for your family may not work for my family, but find a mode of discipline that can help your children be in alignment. That is all that matters.

Chapter 16: Strife and Divide and Rule Members

> Now I plead with you, brethren, by the name of our Lord Jesus Christ, that you all speak the same thing, and *that* there be no divisions among you, but *that* you be perfectly joined together in the same mind and in the same judgment. [11] For it has been declared to me concerning you, my brethren, by those of Chloe's *household*, that there are contentions among you. (1 Corinthians 1:10-11 NKJV)

As with many chapters in this book, this chapter is particularly relevant to pastors and church members—not only pastors' wives. "Divide and rule" members join a church to bring division and confusion at every level of relationships. They want to divide the pastor from their spouse, the pastor from the flock, the flock from the pastor's spouse, and the sheep from other sheep. This is all an effort to control the church or ministry in some way by "hook or crook." These techniques are not only in the corporate world, but Satan has successfully deployed them inside the church to separate mothers from their spiritual children, Naomis from Ruth, fathers from their spiritual children, and mentors from mentees.

In 1 Corinthians, Paul described a situation where the church had contentions, factions, and divisions. Some wanted to identify with Paul. They were his top fans and created a faction devoted to him.

Others sided with Apollos for his eloquence and dynamic preaching. Yet another group who said they were of Christ—He was the only one who could tell them anything. When it comes to strife and division, Paul made it clear that "divide and rule" people are ". . . still carnal. For where *there are* envy, strife, and divisions among you, are you not carnal and behaving like *mere* men?" (1 Corinthians 3:3 NKJV).

Watch out for people who want to create factions or take sides in the church, especially those who side with the pastor to the disrespect and discredit of the pastor's wife. These people are enemies of unity and relationships in a church or ministry. The Bible says we should not be ignorant of the devices the enemy uses to hinder people from hitting the mark of their callings and fulfilling destinies (2 Corinthians 2:11). When you're ignorant, the enemy gains an advantage over you.

Beloved of God, be very careful of people who are one-sided or lean towards the pastor but have hatred or dislike for his wife.

There are reasons why they do this, including:

They know that if you are united as one, they cannot pull down what God is building through both of you.

Remember, "Every kingdom divided against itself is brought to desolation, and every city or house divided against itself will not stand" (Matthew 12:25b NKJV). So, a marriage or ministry divided against itself cannot stand either. The objective of "divide and rule" members is for the marriage and ministry to fall.

Don't side with them, no matter how spiritual they seem. Some pastors complain about their spouse to other women in the church. Male pastors with unchecked egos and pride use other women in the church as sounding boards to complain about their spouse, but it's a setup for a great fall. Pastors, never let another woman think she has an advantage over your wife. It's a foothold the devil will use to bring division and confusion between the two of you and bring the ministry down.

Such people carry Absolom and Delilah spirits. They steal people's hearts, affections, and support so they can stage a coup d'etat and take their seat on the throne by any means necessary. Absolom was David's son but used his beauty and charm to discredit David, steal the hearts of the people, and stab his father in the back.

> Now Absalom would rise early and stand beside the way to the gate. *So* it was, whenever anyone who had a lawsuit came to the king for a decision, that Absalom would call to him and say, "What city *are* you from?" And he would say, "Your servant *is* from such and such a tribe of Israel." ³ Then Absalom would say to him, "Look, your case *is* good and right; but *there is* no deputy of the king to hear you." ⁴ Moreover Absalom would say, "Oh, that I were made judge in the land, and everyone who has any suit or cause would come to me; then I would give him justice." ⁵ And *so* it was, whenever anyone came near to bow down to him, that he would put out his hand and take him and kiss him. ⁶ In this manner Absalom acted toward all Israel who came to the king for judgment. So Absalom stole the hearts of the men of Israel. (2 Samuel 15:2-6 NKJV)

People like Absolom mean no good when they discredit your spouse or listen to your complaints about your spouse. Don't be deceived; they stroke your ego and make you feel good. Delilah made Sampson feel good but eventually used his secret to turn him over to his enemies for destruction. This is what "divide and rule" members do.

It stops the flow of the oil in the ministry.

Once unity is broken, oil will not flow. God will not command a blessing and life forevermore, as stated in Psalms 133, which says:

> Behold, how good and how pleasant *it is* For brethren to dwell together in unity! ² *It is* like the precious oil upon the head, Running down on the beard, The beard of Aaron, Running down on the edge of his garments. ³ *It is* like the dew of Hermon, Descending upon the mountains of Zion; For there the LORD commanded the blessing—Life forevermore. (Psalm 133:1-3 NKJV)

If there is dryness in the ministry, check for division or strife. Power flows where there is unity. Blessings flow where there is unity. The oil of the anointing flows where there is unity.

It is one tactic the kingdom of darkness uses to turn the pastor and the pastor's wife against each other.

Division is a wicked spirit. It brings strife, suspicion, and more. "For where envying and strife is, there is confusion and every evil work" (James 3:16 KJV). The devil loves to bring division because it gives him a break and reprieve from his much-deserved punishment. When pastors and their spouses are divided, he is no longer the target of their unified prayers and efforts to advance the Kingdom of God. Instead, the pastors are now suspicious and cautious of each other and end up targeting each other instead of focusing on the real enemy. No one wins but the devil.

They don't have the divine capacity or capability that the pastor's wife has, so they divide and conquer to discredit her.

They cannot even help the people they confuse to advance in the things of God. They take the focus off themselves by discrediting, undermining, and magnifying the weaknesses of the pastor's wife.

Let me submit to every husband-pastor reading this book that such people are not for you either. Time is what defines their loyalty, devotion, commitment, and friendship. Usually, after such people accomplish their mission or fail at their agenda, they disappear.

Pastors, remember that you have a covenant with your wife. You have no covenant with an assistant, any church member, intercessor, or even the head of the prayer team. Their consistency and durability with your destiny and ministry are undefined, but your wife's consistency and durability are defined by a covenant. As Ruth said, "Where you go, I will go, and where you stay, I will stay. Your people will be my people and your God my God" (Ruth 1:16 NIV).

As pastors, we need to understand that some people are good in the church or ministry but will never get to follow you everywhere because they are not mandated to do so—your wife is. Your relationship with her is the most precious relationship you have on Earth, so protect it from "divide and rule" members. "Therefore what God has joined together, let no one separate" (Mark 10:9 NIV).

Chapter 17: Unforgiveness

"For if you forgive other people when they sin against you, your heavenly Father will also forgive you. But if you do not forgive others their sins, your Father will not forgive your sins." — Jesus in Matthew 6:14-15 NIV

As a pastor's wife, you are at the forefront of ministry and constantly under members' watchful eyes. The enemy targets you for spiritual warfare because you are key to the ministry's success. Your attitude and disposition influence the atmosphere in the ministry. As a result, you will frequently fight the battle of unforgiveness, and it's important for you to understand what it is.

To forgive means to send forth, send away, and denotes letting someone off the hook for whatever they've done.[4] Merriam-Webster's Dictionary defines forgiveness as ceasing to feel resentment against an offender, pardoning, or granting relief from payment. Unforgiveness is holding onto resentment and not letting someone off the hook for what they've done. It can lead to bitterness, wrath, and malice.

---

[4] Blue Letter Bible, "Lexicon :: Strong's G863 – *aphiēmi*," accessed October 9, 2024, https://www.blueletterbible.org/lexicon/g863/kjv/tr/0-1/.

Pastor's wives can face the temptation to hold onto resentment from every imaginable direction, but it often comes from the church members for which you sacrifice—the very people you help and pastor. You may experience betrayal, backbiting, gossip, criticism, loneliness, and more. Your pastor-husband may not defend you the way you expect or may take sides with a church member. That can lead to suffering mentally, emotionally, and spiritually and becoming wounded in one way or another.

Then it becomes hard for you to rise up and say, "I forgive you. Let's move past this." Sometimes, it's a big struggle because it's difficult to go back to a relationship after betrayal. It's hard to resurrect that kind of relationship, even if you have the capability or capacity to do it, so the struggle continues. It can go to the extent that resentment builds up against your pastor-husband and you struggle to forgive him, or conflict arises with your children, and you struggle to forgive them.

Unforgiveness can lead to bitterness and rage. It hinders leaders from becoming effective soldiers in Christ, and a wounded soldier is not a good soldier. Forgiveness must be achieved if they want to become effective warriors in the army of the Lord Jesus Christ, especially in these end times.

We must have the capability to forgive, but we need to pray to God to give us the grace to forgive. There are some things we cannot achieve if we can't forgive. There are some rooms we cannot enter in ministry, even spiritually, if we cannot walk in forgiveness. Many people have failed, not just in ministry but in marriage, because of unforgiveness. So much hurt comes to the pastor and the pastor's wife, but how do you overcome that?

Solutions for Winning the Battle Against Unforgiveness

Understand that betrayal is part of the journey.

Criticism and accusations are just some of the things that may have been used to betray you in the past. Betrayal is a reality of ministry; there will always be a Judas Iscariot, and for your own voice to be catapulted to another level, you need to go through the "Judas experience."

Judas is the way up, not the way down. The "Judas experience" is the way into glory. There is a stepping stone in the spirit called Judas. If you are afraid of it, there are certain levels and dimensions in the spirit you'll not enter. It wasn't until Jesus Christ was betrayed that He fully fulfilled His mandate, assignment, and destiny.

That is part of the spiritual dynamics of the ways of God and how He works. The challenge is to embrace His way. It is painful, and you may feel it's not worth it to forgive, but you must go higher. Behind the betrayal is God's will and purpose for your life. Even Jesus Christ said, "O My Father, if it is possible, let this cup pass from Me; nevertheless, not as I will, but as You *will*" (Matthew 26:39 NKJV). However, Jesus endured the Cross because He knew that the cup of suffering was the only way redemption could come to humanity.

Like Jesus' journey to the Cross, pain, bitterness, and accusation will be a part of your ministry journey. Still, that shouldn't be a reason to drop the ball and say you cannot finish the journey. You have to finish strong. You must finish in power and finish the work and assignment God preordained for you. You can't allow the battle of unforgiveness to make you give up. Commit to forgiveness and healing and keep pressing towards the prize of your high calling in Jesus (Philippians 3:14).

If you do not heal or forgive, you're going to develop bitterness and harsh feelings, and therefore, you're not going to be a very effective pastor's wife. You'll minister from the emotional realm, not the spiritual realm. Your dreams will be from the emotional realm and not from the spiritual realm because you'll be dreaming from your own personal hurt and evil desires against people.

Talk to those who hurt you.

To achieve forgiveness, talk to the people who have hurt you with the goal of reconciliation, especially your spouse, children, and family members. The Scripture says to go to the person who offends you. "Moreover if your brother sins against you, go and tell him his fault between you and him alone. If he hears you, you have gained your brother" (Matthew 18:15 NKJ).

Pray for the grace to forgive.

When you pray, confess your forgiveness for them every single day. Pray the blessing of God upon them. It is not easy to do, but it is biblical. Jesus gave instructions, saying:

> "You have heard that it was said, 'You shall love your neighbor and hate your enemy.' [44] But I say to you, love your enemies, bless those who curse you, do good to those who hate you, and pray for those who spitefully use you and persecute you, [45] that you may be sons of your Father in heaven; for He makes His sun rise on the evil and on the good, and sends rain on the just and on the unjust. (Matthew 5:43-45 NKJV)

Your ability to pray for those who betray you proves you are God's daughter with the DNA of Jesus' blood in your veins. When confronted with betrayers and accusers, David said, "In return for my love they are my accusers, But I *give myself to* prayer" (Psalm 109:4 NKJV).

Get counsel.

Find a counselor to speak with. Some pastors' wives have been hurt but haven't really talked it through with anybody. It's important because you're releasing healing every time you sit down and release the pain, hurt, and despair. So, although you always help others, find someone who can help you talk through things and find healing.

As much as you're supposed to help others, you also need somebody to help you. Every priest has a high priest to report to. Remember that unforgiveness is a weapon the enemy has used to make us ineffective in the realm of the spirit. Educate yourself in the Word of God; fortify yourself with what the Bible says about forgiveness and its benefits. If you don't forgive, Jesus will not forgive you.

CONCLUSION

"I am reminded of your sincere faith, which first lived in your grandmother Lois and in your mother Eunice and, I am persuaded, now lives in you also." – Paul to Timothy in 2 Timothy 2:5 NIV

I pray this book, a labor of love, becomes a life-long resource for you. It's designed to prepare future pastors' wives, encourage and equip current pastors' wives, and educate their husbands and congregation members. Many pastors' wives embark on their journey without a clear understanding of their role in the ministry. Fortunately, section one dispels misconceptions and provides a realistic view of the responsibilities, reminding current pastors' wives of what truly matters.

Make no mistake, being a pastor's wife is hard work. You will juggle being a wife, mother, work, ministry, and more while maintaining your prayer life and relationship with God. You'll face attacks from the enemy and, sometimes, church members. But you cannot give in to their external attacks or an inferiority complex's internal attacks. With the Holy Spirit's help, you must be a rock that can withstand the winds of multiple responsibilities and the waves from the battles you will face. Rocks fix themselves in the Word of God and anchor their lives with the Holy Spirit's help and guidance. He is the best helper.

As a pastor's wife, your role is not about fashion or fame but nurturing the spiritual children God has entrusted to you. Through prayer, intercession, and mothering, focus on helping the saints under your care develop into better Christians. Your impact as a spiritual mother will be immeasurable, and your role in their spiritual development is essential. Embrace this responsibility with confidence because there are things your husband cannot do that only you can.

Paul was persuaded that Timothy's faith had substance and weight because of the godly lives of his grandmother and mother. He was confident that Timothy's faith had been nurtured because of the motherhood legacy that had groomed him. This is the essence of spiritual motherhood and, hopefully, the testimony of the pastors' wives who will read this book and follow its wisdom.

Every pastor's wife must accept her mothering office and responsibility to nurture God's children well. A good mother positively impacts a child's development and instills faith in their hearts. Lois and Eunice exemplify the kind of impact we should all aspire to as spiritual mothers and pastors' wives. Indeed, pastors' wives are not surrogates but nurture and develop the faith of the children in their hands.

Every pastor's wife must be an intercessor. You must pray for yourself, your husband, and your biological children. In the same way that the Holy Spirit is a helper who makes intercession, you must also intercede for your husband as his helpmeet. His weakness is your prayer assignment, and there's no one better to pray for him than you, his covenant partner.

In addition to the office's primary duties, section two also listed the dos and don'ts of a pastor's wife. This is a practical list to add wisdom and knowledge to your journey. You'll be better equipped to handle situations from the lessons learned, experience, and wisdom shared.

In addition to reading books like this one, I want to stress that one of the most excellent "dos" is to heed Paul's requirements for church leaders' wives. He said, "In the same way, the women are to be worthy of respect, not malicious talkers but temperate and trustworthy in everything" (1 Timothy 3:11 NIV). Being a pastor's wife is not about fashion or fame. Paul told Timothy that even if the wives were not already church leaders, the wife of a church leader must be self-controlled, of noble character, and worthy of respect. Paul's list is a tangible starting point for the standard of character necessary for the pastor's wife's office.

No one should take this role lightly. So be sure you seek a mentor with whom you can share your emotional trials, get guidance and advice, and choose your inner circle and prayer partners well. Without them, feelings of isolation and loneliness will amplify. Hopefully, after reading this book, you will be sober about the responsibilities of the role and the battles you will face, but also confident that God chose you and will empower you to flourish. I also believe you are better prepared for the battles of:

1. Accusations
2. Competition
3. Dishonor
4. Famine
5. Gossip and Hypocrisy
6. Jezebels
7. Loneliness
8. Rebellious Children
9. Strife and Divide and Rule Members
10. Unforgiveness

Remember, God gave others victory in these same battles. He can and will do the same for you. And despite the battles, the blessing and spiritual benefits of staying faithful to your office are immense. I pray that God gives you staying power, finishing grace, and mothering grace. I declare you are more than a conqueror.

God is with you and will strengthen you to lead. His opinion matters most, and He says, "The Lord will extend your mighty scepter from Zion, saying, "Rule in the midst of your enemies!" (Psalm 110:2 NIV).

About the Author

Pastor Ritabella is a humble and powerful woman of God who came to know the Lord as a teenager. Through a divine encounter, the Holy Spirit specifically called her to follow Jesus—no human being preached the gospel to her. She started operating in the power of God while she was still just a high school student and has maintained that mantle till today.

Ritabella is a woman of prayer and has been walking the journey of salvation for over twenty years. In 2000, the Lord visited her and bestowed mantles of deliverance, healing, and the prophetic. She also operates in miracles, signs and wonders, and the teaching ministry.

She is the founder and president of Women of Solution International, a mighty, non-compromising women's ministry focused on developing women who convey solutions or answers in various spheres of society, including spiritual, academic, financial, and marital.

She is also a former lawyer, wife to Dr. David Kunobwa, mother of four, and the co-pastor of Rivers of Life Assembly International in Woburn, MA. She travels the globe, taking the gospel of the Lord Jesus Christ to different nations.

For more information, visit www.womenofsolutionintl.org or www.riversoflifeassembly.org.

Made in the USA
Middletown, DE
09 February 2025